The Millennial's Guide to Getting Your Sh*t Together

Catie Hogan

Copyright © 2017 Catie Hogan

ISBN: 9781521998632

Table of Contents

Part III: Essays on Relationships

Congratulations on Getting Your Shit Together!
Resources and Links
Acknowledgements
Let's Be Friends!

Introduction

Hi. I'm Catie Hogan and I wrote this book. A little about me: I'm the founder of Hogan Financial Planning LLC. My business is focused on creating financial plans for Millennials who are hell-bent on taking control of their financial future. I'm also a financial literacy educator and advocate. I teach the fundamentals of personal finance to various groups all over the country. I strongly believe financial literacy is integral to achieving equality and empowering marginalized groups. I've been working in the financial industry for about four years now. In that time I've learned a lot about money, building a career, and myself. My goal is to share those life lessons with you as honestly as possible. I run a blog called *The Funny Financial Planner* (recently renamed *The Get It Together* blog) and I'm a weekly personal finance contributor to *The Scold*. In everything I do, I try to inject humor as often as possible. Learning to navigate adulthood is difficult enough, I don't think it has to be so serious.

In my spare time, I drink a lot of wine, talk to my dog like a human, and write thinly-veiled dick jokes. My satire has been published on cool sites such as *McSweeney's* and *The Belladonna Comedy*. I also write for Sketchworks Comedy in Atlanta and I've had a few of my shorts on *Funny or Die*. If you follow me on Twitter, you know my true passion is critiquing every episode of *The Bachelor*. I have, thus far, made zero dollars from any comedic venture.

I've always wanted to write a book. When I got the idea for *The Millennial's Guide to Getting Your Sh*t Together*, I charged at the project with the motivation and energy of a million Hillary Clintons. Within a few weeks I found myself at a stand still: writing a book is incredibly fucking difficult.

I knew this wasn't going to be easy. I read Amy Poehler's *Yes Please* in which she discusses the immense challenge of writing a book. I didn't really believe her at the time. I thought, "Oh come on, you're just writing your life story and about all the things you love. How hard could it be?"

Poehler was right, as she always is. Holy shit did I underestimate the magnitude of this project. I honestly don't know how people like Stephen King and Nicholas Sparks can just pound out novel after novel after novel. How did Maya Angelou write so many beautiful poems? I'm now in absolute awe of all published authors. Special shout out to the authors who, not only put words on a page, but make them worth reading, too. That's some next-level badassery.

It took me nearly two years to complete this project. As I approached the end of writing, I realized, not only did I want to help young people navigate adulthood, but in a way, I also wanted to write this for me. I wrote the words in each essay to remind myself of my own goals and potential. I need to get my shit together as much as anyone else. Honestly, I don't always have my shit together. I make mistakes on a daily basis. I'm just an ordinary woman trying to do my best. I don't want you to read these essays and think, "who does she think she is?" I want you to read them and say, "Wow, she's relatable and a little fucked up...but I learned something."

One thing I was asked an unsettling amount of times during the writing process was "is your book just for ladies since you talk about feminism and empowerment?" Yes, I've written this book in a secret language only those who identify as female can understand. This is called a "joke" for those who don't speak sarcasm. Still, I understand most of my readers are women, but money, career, and relationship advice is widely applicable no matter how you identify. I'd encourage any dudes reading this to not be embarrassed, there are lessons in here for you too.

Now that you know about the secret lady language I've created in my mind, let me tell you a little about the format of this book. I decided to piece this together in an essay format because, like you, my attention span is that of a distracted goldfish. I also understand not every essay is applicable to your life in this moment. I want you to be able to pick and choose essays as they become relevant to your life. My dream is that you'll refer to this book over the course of several years whenever you need a reminder or a pick me up. I want this to be your go-to reference for all things related to your life both professionally and personally. Or go ahead and read this entire book in one shot and never look at it again. I don't really give a shit as long as I'm receiving royalty checks. That's a lie, I really do care a lot. Thank you so much for purchasing a copy of *The Millennial's Guide to Getting Your Sh*t Together*. I'm honored, I'm flattered, and I'm grateful. That's not a joke. I truly appreciate you.

Why Did I Write This?

My story is similar to millions of Americans who grew up watching *Saved By The Bell* and *Boy Meets World* while posting cheesy song lyrics on AIM. I was a lower middle-class kid with a mom and dad who worked tirelessly to give my younger sister and me a better life. Their only goal was to enable us to pursue our passions and become happy, successful people. They were convinced we'd only achieve our full potential if we graduated from college. Millions of Baby Boomer parents hold these same beliefs for their Millennial children.

I graduated from Emerson College in the midst of a deep recession, with an assload of student loans, and struggling to find gainful employment that would allow me to pay back my debts. I moved back in with my mom and dad and realized I didn't know anything about managing money or how to get my shit together. Does this sound familiar?

When I was a kid, my parents raised us to be hard-working and respectful. I wasn't the top student in my class, but I tried hard. Throughout middle and high school I always made honor roll, played three sports, and participated in as many extracurricular activities as possible. I never wanted to disappoint my parents and I was anxious about what I needed to do to get into a good college. I was a goody two-shoes through and through.

When I decided to attend Emerson College in Boston and major in journalism, my family was thrilled that, together, we had achieved a common goal. I was going to play on the softball team and become the next great Boston sports columnist. Because I had two working and married parents, I didn't get a lot of financial assistance. We weren't well off, but my family made just enough money to disqualify us from a lot of aid. So I took out student loans. Four years later, as I walked across the stage at the Wang Theater, I was aware I had some pretty hefty student debt, but it still hadn't hit me how deep a hole I had actually dug. I was all set to move out west and earn a master's degree at UNLV. I was lucky to receive a graduate assistantship where I could receive a living stipend, work on my thesis, and delay reality for two more years. This was also an opportunity to defer my loans and find a job that paid enough I wouldn't have to eat ramen noodles five days a week. Flash forward two years, I successfully defended my thesis, graduated, and moved back in with my parents in Massachusetts. I had just gotten out of a relationship, again had no job lined up, and was quickly gaining weight for the first time in my life. And then my student loan payment came due. It hit me like a ton of bricks. Where had I gone wrong? I'm an intelligent person. I was an A-B student my entire life. I was a college athlete, a hard worker, I'd completed at least three internships, and always had a part-time job to support myself. What the fuck did I do wrong? The more I asked myself, the more I felt like both a victim and a total moron. Part of this was my fault. I didn't understand the loans I was taking out and I didn't do my due diligence in funding my college education. I also was completely financially illiterate. I didn't know how to save money, budget money, pay bills, or know the ramifications of my financial decisions. That's on me. I am accountable and know I should've been more aware and cognizant of my personal finances. I regret being blissfully ignorant.

At the same time, I felt like the education system had failed both me and my parents. We were sold a false dream: that you must send your child to the best school possible in order for them to have any level of success. My parents come from a different time where working through college allowed you to pay your tuition and expenses. No one helped us with our FAFSA applications and everyone told us, "go ahead, take out those loans."

Not once did I ever learn the basics of personal finance throughout my primary education. I was in the public school system for twelve years, and while I can tell you every tributary to the Mississippi River, and I aced my chemistry acid-base titration lab, not one person taught me how to balance a fucking checkbook. Not once did we discuss the importance of saving for emergencies, or how to set financial goals, or how the stock market works. Not one time.

America has failed its students. I love that we're placing an emphasis on STEM while simultaneously encouraging kids to pursue degrees in the arts. That's terrific, but who the hell is going to teach these kids how to pay taxes and properly allocate the money they've made when they earn their first paycheck? Who the hell is going to teach kids the difference between leasing and buying a car? How are they supposed to know if they're getting fleeced or not? Who the hell is going to teach young adults how a 401(k) works and why tax-sheltered accounts are the greatest tool to building long-term wealth?

Right now the answer is, not a Goddamn person.
Sure, we have to be accountable for our own financial literacy education, but I guarantee you we could solve several economic and social problems by teaching the basics of personal finance skills if we incorporated it into childhood education.

I also want to take a second to tell you I am a white woman from a middle-class family in the suburbs. Although I have known adversity, I am aware of my privilege in this life. While financial illiteracy affects all demographics, I can't begin to know the added societal struggles of minorities and marginalized groups. Throughout these essays, I will do my best to remember we're not all afforded the same opportunities and luxuries in America. My goal is to give as much applicable advice to as many young people as possible, keeping in mind there are inequalities and injustices still plaguing our society. It's well documented that women of color and the LGBTQ+ community face unique issues regarding personal finance and their careers. I know my experience is not ubiquitous, and you may not relate to it at all. My hope is that we will start a financial

6

literacy conversation and figure out how best to teach these fundamental life skills to as many people as we can.

So that's why I'm writing this book: because I'm pissed. I'm pissed at myself, at my education, and at society in general. America has somehow made it possible to mold a smart child into a doctor who doesn't understand the interest rate on their credit cards. This is unacceptable. America has a financial illiteracy epidemic. I'm here to do my part in solving it. I'm here to help you get your shit together.

Young adulthood is hard. It always has been. You'll make your biggest life decisions in your twenties and thirties. If you don't have your shit together, it could cost you personally, professionally, and financially. I don't want to see that happen to anyone.

I wrote this book based on the three areas that impact our lives the most: money, career, and relationships. Money and career are critical cornerstones in the process of getting your shit together. The more you know about how money works in this world, the better you'll be able to control and manipulate it to your advantage. The same goes for career. If you're confident in your ability to negotiate, advance, and maximize employee benefits, you'll be slaying it harder than a topless Khaleesi burning down a tent full of men. I felt it necessary to include essays on relationships as well. I'm not some love guru, but as much as life is about money and a good job, you never really have your shit together until you're surrounded by healthy and fulfilling relationships.

Throughout these essays, I'll share lessons I've learned myself, things I've learned from others, and research I found via Google searches and questionable websites. Maybe my story is a lot like yours. Despite getting fucked over by Sallie Mae, there's still hope for our generation. I want to help you get your shit together, because I want you to know you aren't alone.

We're all that 22 year old frantically searching for a job that doesn't suck the life out of you. We're all that overwhelmed hipster whose rent is the same price as his student loan payment. And we're all that girl on Tinder who's swiped left on 74 consecutive profiles, and whose hope to find a soulmate is dissipating faster than a glacier who just realized climate change is a very real problem.

Don't give up. We're all going to get our shit together... together.

Part I: Essays on Money

Money is the most powerful and influential force in the world. It can be used for good, it can be used for evil, or it can be used for the inconsequential and nonsensical (why do I have subscriptions to three different streaming services?) Money touches everything in our lives. Learning how to manage, grow, and have a positive relationship with our finances is one of the most essential skills a person can develop.

Listen, I'm a woman who likes to learn things the hard way. I'm open about my own past money problems. I graduated college with more debt than I could handle. I spent most of my twenties trying to figure out how to make ends meet. It wasn't until I made financial literacy a priority in my life that my situation began to change. I see so many young people suffering from shame and embarrassment regarding their financial situations. Remember, you are not alone. There are 40 million Americans (and growing) with student loans. The average American household carries more than $16,000 in credit card debt alone. The average college graduate in 2016 finished their degree with more than $37,000 in student loans. And horrifyingly, the average American is dying with more than $62,000 in debt. This is a societal problem and not a *you* problem. So put those feelings of guilt and shame aside and start working toward a better financial future for yourself. You deserve it and the quality of your life depends on it.

I'm on a crusade to end financial illiteracy. I won't get there alone, but if I can do my part in raising awareness and if I can help just one person improve their financial life, then it'll all be worth it. Financial illiteracy in America has reached epidemic proportions. Two-thirds of Americans can't pass a basic financial literacy test. Those numbers are even higher among women and minorities. Thirty-one percent of Americans don't have anything saved for retirement. Twenty-five percent of home loan applications are rejected. We, as a nation, have 2.5 trillion dollars of consumer debt. Since companies began migrating from pension systems to 401(k) plans, the burden of saving for the future moved from the employer to the employee without much notice. Americans are unprepared to lead their own financial lives. Without understanding the basics of how money works in society, how to manage it within your life, and how to save and invest it for the long-term, we are literally putting futures at risk. The sad fact is the only person who will take care of you is you. It's up to us now and we need to do our part to educate ourselves and future generations.

Better Money Management Through Feminism

I don't think I need to tell you, intelligent feminist reader, we have not yet achieved gender equality. We've placed a lot of our efforts into combating the pay gap, shattering glass ceilings, and eliminating discrimination in all walks of life. We're making progress, but it's still not enough. Have no fear though, I've got a new battle plan for us, and it's boring as shit.

Two words: financial literacy. Yup, that's it. We need to be better at handling money. In fact, I believe being good with money will make you an even better feminist. Let me walk you through this tedious topic. I promise to make it more fun and interesting than your last pelvic exam. When I say "be better with money" I'm not just referring to my addiction to Target, or my inability to scan Amazon without purchasing something that will add literally zero value to my life.

Financial literacy and independence have to do with income, savings, retirement, insurance, negotiating, taxes, budgeting, and literally everything your money touches. I know most people would rather pull out their hair than hear me rant about money. But hear me out, this is important. The next step in our crusade for gender equality has to be teaching ourselves, and subsequently the next generation, how to handle their finances like a boss.

Money is power, and power is everything in this world.

Here's a few stats and facts about women and money that'll really grab you by the pu...lady parts. I meant lady parts. Sorry, I'm in a locker room right now and there's a scary orange creamsicle man with a comb-over trying to kiss me.

1. According to the National Capability Study performed by the Financial Industry Regulatory Authority (FINRA), two-thirds of Americans couldn't pass a basic financial literacy

test. As poorly as men tested, they still scored 16% better than women.

2. Prudential published a study in 2015 which found 75% of women believe having enough money to maintain their lifestyle in retirement is very important, but only 14% felt confident they would be able to do so.

3. The same study showed only 41% of women said they understand stocks and bonds compared to 56% of men.

4. Women, on average, make 20% less than men. "But we already know this, Catie!" Well, think about the long-term effect of earning 20% less. This inequality is exponentially magnified over time.

5. Women are the primary victims of financial abuse. Financial abuse is most often seen in situations of domestic violence. If you're unfamiliar with this horrifically common tactic, abusers manipulate victims' money to keep them under the abuser's control. It's nearly impossible for a woman who has been saddled with debt and/or who is lacking funds to free herself from this type of abuse.

6. Women have a longer life expectancy than men. So for all you ladies letting your dudes handle the money, there's a very solid chance at some point in your life you will be the sole financial manager for your family.

7. Women who lack financial knowledge are at greater risk to acquire large amounts of debt, have poor credit, lower salaries, and experience difficulty managing incomes, investments, and taxes.

Financial literacy (being good with your money) is the next important step for feminism. In order to fix the issues outlined above, we must snatch our finances by the coin sack and educate ourselves.

Every day women bravely face institutionalized issues that we, as a nation, are still working to correct. But as women, we need to do what we can to help ourselves. Handling your finances like a badass will assist in setting you up for success in all your future endeavors, be it professional or personal.

So here's a list of reasons why I think learning about money will make you a better feminist:

You'll Be Moving the Needle

Yas, Queen, you'll be pushing us closer to equality. When your budget's on point, you're contributing to your retirement plan, and negotiating for the salary you deserve, you are advocating for women's rights whether you know it or not.

Independent Ladies are the Baddest Bitches

Destiny's Child sang about this in the early 2000s. So Beyoncé, how do you become independent? You learn how to properly manage money. There's a plethora of books, online tools, and resources to help you learn the basics of budgeting, investing, etc. Independent women are the future of this nation. When you're financially independent, you'll have greater resources at your disposal to fight for causes you believe in.

You'll Feel Like Wonder Woman

Financial intelligence is empowering and a confidence booster. You'll impress the pants off your lovers and friends with your savvy skills. You'll develop a slight swagger to your walk. You'll start wearing fake glasses and a top knot to appear more intellectually inclined. Your confidence and empowered aura will rub off on those around you. This is good for all of society.

You'll Be Less Likely to Loan Money to Your Ex

Financial literacy leads to better decisions. Which means you're less likely to loan shitty people money, rack up your credit card for dumb reasons, or make impulsive purchases (i.e. the kayak sitting in my garage).

Unleash Your Inner Oprah

Believe it or not, how you handle your personal finances directly impacts the young ladies in your life. Whether you've got daughters, nieces, or younger sisters you'll be setting an example for the next generation with your badassery. You'll be an inspiration, and that, my friends, is feminist as fuck.

So go ahead, Lady Boss, make that money. Then save it, invest it, and spend it wisely. The little girl standing behind you is watching in admiration.

This essay first appeared on The Scold *on October 19, 2016*

How to Actually Become Financially Literate

Oh, what's that you say? You're inspired now? And you're jumping out of your yoga pants to find out how to actually become a badass with your money? Awesome. I'm glad you're on board. If I haven't convinced you of the importance of financial literacy yet, you're dead to me. Sorry, that was a bit harsh.

You could spend years studying economics and finance at a prestigious university, or you can read the listicle I'm about to provide you. My hope is you'll take the information I'm laying on you and put it into action. I'll bet you a Chipotle burrito (my favorite), that if you do everything mentioned in this listicle you will be financially literate.

As you conquer this list you'll find yourself morphing into a more bold and spectacular version of yourself. Embrace your newfound power.

Books I've Read Not Written By E.L. James

We've got to start with some must-reads. I've read a ton of personal finance books. I needed something to cool me off in between each installment of the *Fifty Shades* series. Most financial books will bore you to tears. Here are a few that are palatable and super informative:

The Total Money Makeover by Dave Ramsey

This book is great for people in debt (student loans, credit cards) and those who really need help getting their finances in control. I'm not a big Dave Ramsey fan per se. He's a little too "in your face" for my taste, but his book really does a nice job of simplifying personal finance. Ramsey is brutally honest about the dumb stuff people do with their money and he'll whip your debt-ridden ass into shape in no time.

The Millionaire Next Door by Thomas J. Stanley & William

What are the habits of the wealthy? What do they invest in? How do they save? What kinds of jobs do they work? This is such an interesting read because it really digs deep into the habits and mindsets of everyday people who are great at accumulating wealth. It's not the most exciting book, but you'll learn a lot.

Think and Grow Rich by Napoleon Hill

This is an oldie but a goodie. The title sounds gimmicky and like a weird scam, but this is truly a fascinating book on financial and personal success. Napoleon Hill dedicated an absurd amount of his life to studying America's most influential men. He then took what he learned and developed the 13 principles for success. Remember, this book was written a long- ass time ago, so just ignore and/or roll your eyes at the outdated language but pay attention to the valuable lessons.

The Money Book for the Young, Fabulous & Broke by Suze Orman

If you haven't seen Kristen Wiig's impression of Suze Orman, please take a minute to YouTube it. This book is great for the new college grad or someone in their first job. Orman totally gets what kind of struggles young people face and she'll provide you with some actionable steps to follow. I don't agree with 100% of her teachings — some of her ideas seem counterintuitive — but she's still a smart lady boss who's worth reading.

Where Have All the Dollars Gone?

I know you're probably feeling like a student overwhelmed by your class "required reading" list right now. Remember those days? My biggest concern was how I'd finish 75 pages of reading and still make it to Thirsty Thursday festivities at my local dive bar. I long for those simple times.

The common denominator throughout each recommended book is that every dollar you earn needs to have a job.

Without knowing it, you've already assigned each of your dollars a job, but maybe not the right one. These "jobs" include paying bills, investing, saving, and other various expenditures (for my hometown friends, this includes your copious spending on wine and weed). I recommend using a budgeting app to keep track of your dollars.

Here's a list of budgeting tools that are user friendly and will help you get your dollar "employees" in line:

Mint

I personally use Mint and I do enjoy its simplicity and usefulness. Mint requires you input your bank account information, and I know a lot of people are wary of this. Mint does take cyber security and encryption seriously. They're aware if they don't protect consumer information, they'll be out of business tomorrow. Mint allows me to see all of my accounts in one place. I can easily track my spending, set goals, monitor my progress, and find ways to improve. It's a cool tool to see your overall financial "big picture". It's also free, so that's nice.

You Need a Budget

I've heard a lot of good things about You Need a Budget (YNAB). Again, this tool is all about knowing where you spend your money and giving every dollar you earn a job. YNAB is best suited for people in debt. The goal of YNAB is to get you out of the red and saving more.

GoodBudget

GoodBudget is another tool that has received positive reviews. Basically, this app digitizes the old school budgeting method of labeling envelopes ("transportation," "food," "utilities," etc.) and digitally places a set amount of cash in each envelope per month. GoodBudget will help you get organized and in control of your spending.

Get Your Shit Together (Get Organized)

Organization within my house and office prevents me from morphing back into my true self: a chaotic messy bitch. Personally, I think organizing your financial documents is the worst step simply because it's a pain in the ass. Yet, your effort will be worth the tediousness. I want you to take one hour per month to organize your financial documents and to track your accounts. This doesn't have to be a super detailed process. Get a few manila folders and organize your financial documents by category (bills, investment accounts, bank accounts, retirement accounts, receipts, etc.). There's something about decluttering and organizing that clears my mind. I hope it does the same for you. More importantly, when your financial life is organized it'll provide a sense of clarity regarding your current money status. This in turn will assist you in making more informed financial decisions. You're more susceptible to costly mistakes when your personal finances are in disarray. The simple act of organizing can save you from bad decisions. I suggest putting on your favorite music and eating a snack during this step. I personally eat a lot of Babybel cheese when I organize.

Date Night

People think I'm crazy for this one, but hear me out. So often money is a source of strife and it is a common cause of divorce. I believe there are ways to change that. I want money discussions to be a source of happiness. So here's what I'm proposing: tell your spouse/significant other you are having a once-per-month financial date night. Stop laughing. I'm not kidding. Prepare yourself; this is going to lead to some passionate lovemaking. If you're single, you can still follow these steps, although I wouldn't recommend

a financial date for someone you just picked up on Tinder.
Step 1: Make or order a romantic dinner. For me, this means
a Domino's mushroom pizza with a side of Tums.

Step 2: Pop open a bottle of wine or your favorite craft
beers. Personally, I enjoy turning my mouth bright red
with a cheap cab sauv.
Step 3: Talk to your significant other about this past month's
income and expenses. DO NOT blame one another for going
over budget or impulse buys. Be calm and collected when
talking about monthly expenditures. Remember, resentment
will not get you laid. Try this instead: discuss each of your
financial strengths and what you think YOU need to improve
upon. Accountability is SO hot.

Step 4: Set goals. There's nothing sexier than writing
down your short-term (can be accomplished within a
year), intermediate (1-5 years), and long-term goals (5+
years) as a couple. Be as specific as possible. Goal setting
is the new foreplay, y'all.

Step 5: This step kind of goes hand-in-hand with the short-
term goal setting, but I want you and your special person to
each decide on one thing you can do better next month.
Perhaps you want to bring in an extra $500 with a side hustle.
Maybe your partner can bring their lunch to work during the
week. Again, write it all down and put it up on your fridge so
you can hold yourselves accountable.

Step 6: You are now full of pizza, wine, and love. Your
finances are in order and it didn't cause a screaming match.
There is peace in your home. We both know what happens
next. You and your love climb into bed and declare you're
too tired for sex.

Get Some Help

Professional financial advice can be life changing. I know
what you're thinking. People who work in finance cannot be
trusted! They are the scum of the earth! Unfortunately, there

have been plenty of bad apples and shady business practices that scared away people who could truly benefit from financial planning. The bad apples also make it much more difficult for the good and honest planners to gain the trust of clients (*cough cough me cough cough*).

Here's the deal: there are good financial planners in the world who honestly want to help you. So how do you find these people? First, look for advisors/planners who are "fee-only" and have taken a "fiduciary oath." Most of the time, these people will also be Certified Financial Planners (CFP). First and foremost, CFPs and planners who hold themselves out as fiduciaries are held to much higher standards than other financial professionals. The term "fiduciary" means a person who legally and ethically is obligated to act in your best interest. "Fee-only" means the planner doesn't make their money from commissions and you pay them directly. Essentially, these people won't be tempted to sell you crappy investments and products for personal gain.

Becoming financially literate takes a bit of commitment as well as a willingness to learn and make adjustments in your life when needed. These few simple steps should help you get on your way.

This essay first appeared on The Scold *on October 26, 2016*

Shit You Should Probably Know: A Financial Glossary Best Served with Wine

I recently co-hosted a "Women, Wine & Financial Wisdom" night with a really awesome friend of mine who's a financial planning superstar. She and I share a passion for teaching financial literacy and empowering women with money, so we spent weeks planning and plotting our inaugural event. Would anyone even come? What are we going to talk about? How many glasses of wine should we drink before the guests arrive? How can we be funny and informative and not a snooze fest? We resigned ourselves to the fact that, if all else failed, at least we provided free alcoholic beverages and appetizers on a Wednesday night.

Our goal for the evening was to employ the most entertaining and educational strategies to teach these lovely ladies about personal finance. We already knew the women in attendance were confident and independent Beyoncés, so our hope was for each of them to leave feeling more empowered and motivated to handle their money.

The idea of teaching financial literacy in a live event format is new to me. Typing witty articles is far easier than being engaging in real life. I can't even get my dog to listen to me, much less a room filled with brain-wielding humans. My personal short-term goal is to become a better public speaker. Ultimately, I'd like to be able to talk to large groups without breaking out into hives #DreamBig.

I've since reflected on what went well, what could've gone better, and that everyone is better off if I'm not the one providing the baked goods. The brownies I made for the party were so hard they should've been registered as deadly weapons. I'm like the Buffalo Bills of the kitchen, I always try hard but consistently come up a little short.

We received tons of helpful feedback I'm sure I'll forget

to implement during my next financial literacy seminar. One common theme among the women at the event (but probably also women in general?) was a sense of not wanting to ask "stupid questions." Although there are

definitely stupid questions in life, if it's related to any sort of personal finance or money topic, it's not dumb. Your financial questions are never stupid because your future depends on you actually knowing the answer. So the next time you feel like your money inquiry is embarrassing just know someone on Twitter once asked "What's Obama's last name?" What I'm saying is just ask your damn question.

For many people, their "stupid question" is wanting to know the definition of a financial term. I'm talking about terms you hear on the regular. Like when people talk about their 401(k). What's the actual definition of a 401(k)? Is it different than a pension or a 403(b)? These aren't stupid questions by any stretch and it's important that you ask or type it into the Google machine if you don't know the answer.

So here's what I'm going to do. I'm going to give you some of the most common financial terms. This is in no way a complete or comprehensive glossary. This is my attempt to provide you a basic understanding of some terms you should know. Print this article out, carry it with you, memorize it, or just give it a glance and maybe learn something new. You may know all of these terms. You may not know any. I don't know your life! I simply hope this moves your needle a tiny bit closer to financial independence and freedom.

This glossary is also not in alphabetical order because who has time for that shit? Also, I just wrote these words as they came to me. Sorry about it. My dream is that you'll read this entire glossary and then yell "I'm financially lit, bitch!" To learn more about each of these terms, I've included resources and links in the "Resources and Links" section at the end of the book.

23

Stock - If you own stock, you own a piece of a company. Companies need investors for various reasons so sometimes they issue "shares" of stock. If you buy 100 shares of XYZ Company's stock, and they've issued a total of 1 million shares, then congratulations, you own .0001% of XYZ Company!

Bond - A bond is when you lend your money, for a certain period of time, to either a company or a form of government (could be local, state, or federal). In return, you'll receive interest for being so nice and lending your money to them. Bonds are used to fund various projects and initiatives.

Warning: Bonds are more complex than this. This is the ultimate simplification and basic definition.
Dividend - When you own shares of a company, that company may pay out a sum of money to you on, usually, a quarterly basis. This sum of money is called a dividend. You can reinvest the dividends or take the money and run. By reinvesting the dividends, you'll get to see the magic of compounding interest over time.

Mutual Fund - A mutual fund gathers up a big group of investors — like me and you — pools their money, and uses that sum to invest in a bunch of different companies via stocks, bonds, etc. Why do this? Couple of reasons. First, it makes investing in multiple assets much cheaper. Secondly, It's important not to put all your eggs in one basket when investing. We call spreading our eggs (money) into different baskets (investments) "diversification." There are all kinds of mutual funds out there. They differ by goals, investment types, minimums, expenses, etc.

ETF - This stands for exchange traded fund and they've gained a ton of popularity in recent years. "Exchange traded" means you can buy and sell these funds like a stock on an exchange. ETFs track indexes (S&P 500 for example), or commodities (think gold and grains), bonds, or index funds. ETFs are cool because they often have lower fees than mutual funds and are liquid (which means you can sell your ETF and quickly convert it to cash). Like the previous definitions, there's more to it than this, but as of this writing I've had far too much coffee and need a bathroom break. Talk amongst yourselves.

Traditional IRA - Ok, I'm back. A Traditional Individual Retirement Account (IRA) is a tax-deferred way to save for your future. Basically, you contribute pre-tax dollars, invest those dollars, and watch them grow. You don't pay taxes on the money in the IRA until you withdraw it in retirement. IRAs are a great vehicle for growing your money over the long-term.

Roth IRA - A Roth IRA is a fun way to save for retirement as well. Roth IRAs are different than Traditional in that, instead of contributing pre-tax dollars, you're putting in after-tax dollars. The money you contribute this year is not tax deductible, but the contributions will grow tax-free and will be withdrawn tax- free when you retire.

*There are limitations and rules you should be aware of regarding both Traditional and Roth IRAs (i.e. contributions, income, age, conversions, etc.) Be sure to know your options and check with a financial planner before making a decision about retirement accounts.

401(k) - This is a retirement savings plan provided by your employer. The money you contribute will grow tax-deferred. Many employers choose to match your contributions up to a certain percentage to help your money grow even more. Yay, free money! When you withdraw money in retirement, it'll then be taxed at your ordinary income tax rate.

403(b) - Similar to a 401(k), the 403(b) is most commonly the retirement savings plan for public school teachers, non-profit employees, and ministers. There are 457 plans, as well. Those are usually for government workers.

Pension - You've got to love pensions. It's a retirement account where your employer makes the contributions on your behalf. How nice! Because pensions cost the company a lot of money, employers are moving away from them and shifting the onus of saving for retirement to the employee, à la the 401(k). If you do have a pension, it's important to know what kind and the details.

Life Insurance - There are two main types of life insurance: term and permanent (whole life). Term insurance lasts for a certain amount of time (usually 10, 20, or 30 years). Permanent insurance is as it sounds: permanent. Having enough life insurance is super important if you have a spouse or children relying on your income. For the vast majority of people, there's no need for whole life insurance. There are plenty of term insurance policies available to cover your needs for a fraction of the price.

Interest Rate - This is the amount the lender charges a borrower for use of the lender's money. You could be either the borrower or the lender. Interest rates can be fixed, which means the interest rate doesn't fluctuate over the period of the loan. Or it can be variable meaning the interest rate fluctuates.

Simple Interest - Simple interest is a method to calculate the interest owed on a loan. To calculate simple interest multiply the loan amount by the interest rate by the number of days between each loan payment. This method is most often used by automobile loans, personal loans, and sometimes mortgages to calculate what is owed.

Compound Interest - This is as close to magic as it gets. If you put $1,000 in an account earning 10% annually, at the end of one year you'd have $1,100, right? So for year two, you're now earning interest on top of the original interest. Your new $1,100 balance will earn the 10% and, at the end of year two, the account will be worth $1,210. Same for year three: now you're earning 10% interest on $1,210. See how that works? The trick is this: the greater number of "compounding periods," in this case years, the greater the amount of compound interest you will accrue. This is how you boost your savings over a longer period of time. Math is magic!

Adjusted Gross Income (AGI) - This is a common term around tax time (which feels like it's always right around the corner. Gah! No! Puke!) Gross income is simply the sum of all the income you earned in a year. From there, you'll subtract your deductions (the most common include business expenses, medical expenses, alimony, retirement plan contributions, and losses from a sale of property). Gross income - Deductions = Adjusted Gross Income. After your AGI is calculated, you can then apply the standard federal deductions to find out your total taxable income. Isn't tax preparation the best!? Are we having fun yet? Do accountants even have friends?

Standard Deduction - This is the dollar amount you can subtract from your Adjusted Gross Income. It helps make sure at least part of your income is not taxable. Isn't the IRS generous and sweet? The amount you are allowed to deduct depends on your filing status, age, if you're disabled and/or are claimed on someone else's tax return as a dependent. Remember, you can't use the standard deduction if you itemize. We could easily fall into a tax rabbit hole here, but I like you too much as a reader and do not wish to inflict any further pain upon you.

I've been working on this glossary all day and I'm pooped. Did you yell "I'm financially lit, bitch!"? Please say yes, otherwise all this work was for naught.

This essay first appeared on The Scold *on January 10, 2017*

Goal Setting Like a Champ

I spent years asking myself one question over and over: "What do I want?" My immediate answer usually involves some sort of ice cream. For the majority of my life, my long-term answer was: "I have no idea" or "A lot of different things, depending on the day." My personality is one of great curiosity. I fall in love with different interests and hobbies often. I can only intensely focus on one subject for short spurts. I was never the kind of kid who knew from age five what they wanted to be when they grew up. It took me a really long time to accept this about myself and when I finally did, I realized I'm not alone.

Here's a quick list of careers I've considered pursuing since kindergarten, in no particular order:
1. Meteorologist
2. Storm chaser
3. Talk show host
4. Carpenter
5. Professional basketball player
6. Sports journalist
7. Professional golfer
8. Sabermetrics analyst
9. Author
10. Cartoonist
11. Stockbroker
12. Financial planner
13. Financial literacy educator
14. Exotic dancer
15. Ice cream flavor inventor
16. Magician
17. Landscaper
18. Comedian
19. Founder of a cult
20. Astronaut

When I finally grasped the true core of my personality, I was then able to deeply examine what I want in this life on a a personal and professional level. It's important to not only set long-term life goals, but also short-term goals you can accomplish this week, month, and year. Short-term goals are little miracle workers. When you check a short-term goal off your list, you'll get an instant boost of confidence. It'll help re- energize you in continuing your pursuit of the next, greater goal. Short-term goals are all about building and sustaining momentum to see you through your long-term aspirations.

So let's start small. How do we do this? It's critically important to set measurable and attainable short-term goals. First and foremost, you need to get yourself a goal sheet. What's a goal sheet you ask? Well, it can be a piece of computer paper, notebook paper, a Post-It note, a whiteboard, a chalkboard; I don't give a shit what you use just find something you can write on and hang it in a place where you'll see it each and every day.

On this goal sheet, you will write down your short, intermediate, and long-term goals. Repeat after me: WRITE IT DOWN. I'm not just saying this for shits and giggles. There are studies that show people who write their goals down and look at them each day are more likely to achieve them. I find it helps keep me focused when I get distracted. I am distracted approximately 75% of every waking moment. Start by setting a goal for today. It could be as simple as "organize office," or "finish a chapter of book," or "don't yell into the void." Whatever you choose, make sure it's attainable today. Then give yourself a deadline: "I need to have my office organized by 4 P.M." When you complete what may seem like a menial task, reward yourself and physically cross it off from your goal sheet.

Repeat the process of setting and achieving daily goals for a week or two. Then start setting weekly and monthly objectives to really get into a goal-oriented mindset. As you continue to achieve the small goals, begin to think about intermediate and long-term aspirations. Intermediate is defined as achievable within 1-5 years. Long-term is five or more years away.

When you begin to formulate these longer-term goals, really evaluate your values, priorities, and what would truly make you happy. Simply stating you want to be rich, or buy a house, or retire is not enough. We need to make these goals SMART: specific, measurable, attainable, reasonable, and time-based.

We need to make your lofty ambitions quantifiable because it's the only way we can then begin to formulate a plan and measure progress. Does that make sense? Good. If not, just think of it this way: we're painting a picture of your future and the more color and detail we can add, the better it'll be. So if your goal is to be rich, then ask yourself, how much money does that mean? How much income will I need to generate each year? How much will I have to save and invest? How long do I have to reach this goal?

I really want you to spend time contemplating your long-term objectives. I realize I just said goals should be "reasonable" as one of the parameters, but I think that applies more to short and intermediate goals than long-term ones. Don't be afraid to dream big. In my humble opinion, if your dreams don't scare you, they're not big enough. You may be embarrassed or nervous to write down an "unrealistic" long-term goal, but fucking go for it. History has proved the craziest of dreamers are the most successful. You too can make a janky sex tape and turn it into a billion dollar media and beauty product empire.

So what happens when you set lofty long-term goals and don't reach them quite like you hoped? It's okay! Put a positive spin on it. If your goal was to have a million dollars by the time you turned 50, and you only were able to save $750,000. Well that's $750,000 you might not have had if you didn't set that SMART goal in the first place.

The point here is to try. Your future is too important and you deserve all the best life has to offer. So set your sights high, and even if you come up a little short, you will be better off than if you hadn't tried at all.

Where to Begin When You Don't Know Where to Begin

So what's the most common thing I hear among financially frustrated friends, family, and clients? Other than, "You have something stuck in your teeth," it's always some variation on this sentence: "I don't even know where to start."

Usually people will say this when they feel overwhelmed, confused, and truly unsure of how to begin the journey toward financial independence. What's the answer then? Normally I say, "It depends," because it really does, but I don't want you to start throwing tomatoes and booing me, so I'll try to give a generally applicable answer.

Inventory Time

I believe the best place to start regaining control of your money is by taking inventory. First, make a list: everything you own vs. everything you owe (assets vs. liabilities). Then make another list: all the income you make in a month vs. all the money you spend in a month (income vs. expenses). Really break these lists down as much as you can, the more specific the better. Why spend the time and effort to write all this down or put it in a spreadsheet? It's going to paint a clearer picture of your overall financial situation. It's also going to get you on the path to organization. It'll be easier to make decisions regarding a financial plan for the future if you've got an organized view of your "big picture."

The Truth Hurts

So what comes next? Another task for you! Write down your biggest financial pain points. Is it student loans? Credit card debt? Overspending? Don't write, "I don't have enough money." That's not going to solve anything. Why don't you have enough money? Are your bills overwhelming? Is your housing too expensive? Are your transportation costs eating away at your budget? Take the time to figure out what's costing you the most. Here's the difficult part: you're going to need to be your own biggest critic. What are you wasting money on? There's a huge difference between things we actually need and things we really want. Be brutally honest with yourself and your wasteful expenditures. Again, list them all.

Set Your Sights High

So how do you make lasting and positive financial change? You need a plan, ya goober. First you need goals. Short-term goals, intermediate-term goals, and long-term goals. Specific, Measurable, Attainable, Reasonable, and Time-Based (SMART) goals are the gold standard. For the millionth time, you better write them down. Now figure out what small changes you can make today, this week, this month, and this year. If you cancel one subscription this week, can you then apply that money to paying off a credit card or saving for a vacation? Can you pick up a couple of overtime shifts this month or cut back on lunches out? These small sacrifices now will make a big difference over the course of time.

Take It Further

So now you're on the right path. You've done a great job thus far, young Padawan. This is the part where it may get a little more complicated and involved. Now you need to start a savings and investing plan for the future. Begin by evaluating your work's retirement plan. Are you contributing enough to receive your company's match, if one is offered? Can you contribute more? Perhaps you should look at opening a Roth or Traditional IRA. Begin thinking about automating your savings. Choosing investments and which savings accounts to utilize for optimal results can be overwhelming. If you don't feel confident, then do your due diligence and research what may be best for you. If you find yourself not understanding or with more questions, then you can probably guess what I'm going to recommend. Talk to a financial planner. Find someone who upholds a fiduciary standard, good ethics, and has a great reputation. A good planner will help you establish, implement, and monitor your progress in reaching financial goals. We're entering a new age in financial planning where practitioners are actually eager to work with young adults. Financial planning is not just for rich middle-aged dudes anymore either.

There you have it, a starting point when you don't even know where to begin. Not everyone will begin this journey in the same place, but you won't regret taking that first step toward financial independence.

This essay first appeared on The Scold *on February 14, 2017*

Emergency Funds for When You Can't Even

One Thursday evening not too long ago, I could not even.
I could not. So I poured myself a glass of wine. I put away
my laptop. I caught up on the 800 shows I've started
watching since subscribing to <u>Hulu</u>. I needed a moment of
peace to myself. The universe seemed to be conspiring
against me. Everything that could go wrong on this
particular Thursday did go wrong. I felt like life wasn't
just *giving* me lemons, it was pelting me in the head with
them.

I know we all have these days; I'm no special unicorn. This
got me thinking about the whole "when it rains it pours"
phenomenon. Why is it that bad stuff happens in clusters?
Doesn't it seem like when your car shits the bed, all of a
sudden your house needs random repairs, and your dog gets
sick from eating the Halloween candy you accidentally left
out? You say to yourself, "Why is this all happening at
once!?"

While you are hanging on to any sliver of sanity, you're also
realizing your bank account is about to take a big hit. You
feel compelled to ball up in a corner, hide away from the
world, and watch 15 reruns of *Friends* in a row (this can't be
just me, you guys). Unfortunately, this is not a good solution
to your problems. Crappy things are going to happen in life
and there isn't much we can do about it, right? I say wrong!

What we can do is prepare ourselves. You know if it's got
tires or a penis it's going to give you problems (that's how
the saying goes, right?). So why not take the necessary
precautions to lessen the blow of life's punches? This is
where an emergency fund comes in handy.

Everyone needs an emergency fund. Ideally, you will have
3-6 months worth of expenses saved in a separate savings
account that you only touch in case of — yup, you guessed
it — emergencies. If you don't have the cash on hand to

fully fund an emergency account, start small. Put away $5, $10, $20 a month until you get to $500 or $1000. This will be your safety net when you plummet from life's high wire.

You know eventually you're going to need to call a plumber for a leaky toilet on the same day you break your ankle attempting to keep up with your friend, Erin, in Zumba class. What the hell, Erin? I told you I'd look like a drunk baby on the dance floor. Fuck you and your perfect J.Lo choreography. In these rare situations, wouldn't it be nice if you had an emergency fund to cover the unexpected? Your emergency fund may not cover all of the expenses, but it can ease at least part of the pain.

I'm an annoyingly optimistic person, but I'm also a realist. I don't sit around waiting for the other shoe to drop, but in the off-chance it does, I want to limit its impact. Now that I've ruined your day by reminding you about life's ability to bitch slap you at any moment, go ahead and get your emergency fund started.

Your emergency fund should take precedence over any other financial goals. You should establish an emergency account before retirement, investing, and vacation funds. It's also imperative to remember, credit cards are not emergency funds. Using a credit card in an emergency is a financial trap you'll be hard pressed to climb out of. An emergency fund should be cash or cash equivalents only (a money market is a good emergency fund cash equivalent). A fully funded emergency account can save you a world of hurt.

This essay first appeared on The Scold *on November 2, 2016*

Answers to Your Most Embarrassing Financial Questions

I reached out to a bunch of friends and asked them to send me their most "embarrassing" money related questions. I put those words in quotations because, the truth is, there aren't any embarrassing or stupid money questions. Don't be ashamed of what you don't know. Swallow your pride and find out the answer; your financial future depends on it. All of the questions I received were legitimate and relatable. I'm truly proud of everyone who sent me a question. I hope their bravery in asking will inspire you all.

Let's jump right in:

"I think my company offers the option to buy their stock but I don't know if it's discounted, how much I should buy, when I should sell it, and how long I should let it grow."

Great question from a young bad bitch. First, let me ask you this: is your company offering an Employee Stock Purchase Plan (ESPP) or stock options? Ask your benefits manager if you aren't sure! With an Employee Stock Purchase Plan your employer is providing you the opportunity to purchase company stock, usually at a discount ranging from 5%-15%. On the other hand, stock options give the employee the right to purchase the company's stock at a fixed price for a certain period of time. The cost is usually what the stock was valued at when the option was granted. There are two types of stock options, so it's important to know exactly what your employer is offering. Do not be afraid to ask!

Taking advantage of a company's ESPP or stock options can be a good way to build long-term wealth. You don't want to put all your metaphorical eggs into your company's basket though. A diversified portfolio is crucial for investing success, so make sure the company stock you purchase works well within your greater financial picture. Owning too much company stock can be an issue.

If you do decide to purchase your company's stock either through an ESPP or stock options, it's important to understand the different tax implications. I would get into tax consequences, but this essay is going to be long enough. In the "Resources and Links" section at the end of the book, I've included a good article that you can read to learn more about common stock plan mistakes. Be sure to check it out.

"I have some bonds that have reached maturity...but I have no idea what a bond is. What am I supposed to do with them?"

Let me define "bond" before we continue. A bond, in the simplest terms, is money you are letting a government entity or company borrow for a certain period of time to fund their projects and initiatives. In return, they will pay you interest. There's a lot more to bonds than I care to write about, but when you get a minute, *Investopedia* does a good job at explaining how bonds work. I've included a link to *Investopedia*'s explanation of bonds in the "Resources and Links" section.

After speaking with this friend, we discovered what she had in her possession were savings bonds received as a kid (you know the ones grandma and grandpa give you on your birthday or around the holidays). The savings bonds matured and she doesn't know what to do with them. This is so common. I hear similar versions of this question all the time.

For this particular friend, I would say her best choice is to redeem the savings bonds at the bank and reinvest the proceeds. Your savings bonds, while a low-risk investment, likely have underperformed in the stock market in the last few decades. I suggest reinvesting in index funds or ETFs within a Roth IRA to maximize future growth. She may also want to use the money to pay off any credit or student loan debt.

Remember, everyone's risk tolerance, risk capacity, time-horizon, and financial situation are different so be sure to consult with a financial planner or do your research before choosing any investments. Also, when you redeem your savings bonds, it counts as income that you'll have to report on your taxes that year. In the "Resources and Links" section I've included a useful article on what to do with your old savings bonds.

"What's a 401(k)?"

Another solid question, young polliwog. The term "401(k)" refers to the Internal Revenue Code's subsection 401(k), which lays out the details and requirements for employer-sponsored defined-contribution retirement plans. "Defined-contribution" means the employee is contributing money to the plan. Now, there are a few types of 401(k)s, but generally speaking, the 401(k) is a tax-deferred account to save money for your retirement. Again, tax-deferred means the money you put into the account won't be taxed until you withdraw it in retirement. All your contributions and earnings within the 401(k) will grow without having to worry about annual taxes. A 401(k) allows you to invest money contributed directly from your paycheck before taxes.

So, why should you participate in your employer's 401(k) plan? Because, it's the best way to save money for retirement. Taxes eat away at your investment earnings. By contributing to a 401(k), you are sheltering your contributions and subsequent earnings from the IRS until you withdraw them in retirement. When you're at least 59 1/2 years old, and decide to start withdrawing your 401(k) funds, you will then be taxed at your ordinary income tax rate.

You can contribute up to $18,000 per year into your 401(k) as of 2017. The amount you choose to contribute is generally a percentage of your paycheck. You'll let your employer know how much to withdraw ahead of time.

As mentioned earlier, there are a few variations on the 401(k). If you have questions, be sure to ask your HR department or get your hands on an employee manual and do your research. I've included a link for more information on 401(k) plans in the "Resources and Links" section.

"What's the difference between a Traditional IRA and a Roth IRA?"

Another important question, from the same little polliwog friend. So first of all, IRA stands for Individual Retirement Account. A Traditional IRA is an account where you're contributing pre-tax money. The contributions you make are tax deductible at both the federal and state level in the current year. The money will then grow over time (of course you have to pick good investments within the IRA) without having to deal with federal income taxes each year. When you withdraw the money in retirement, that's when it'll be taxed at your ordinary income tax rate.

A Roth IRA is an account where the money you contribute is considered after-tax, meaning you will pay income taxes on the money in the year you contribute it. Contributions to a Roth IRA are not tax deductible. The money in the Roth IRA will grow tax-free. Unlike the Traditional IRA, when you withdraw the money in retirement, it will remain tax-free, because you already paid taxes in the year in which you made the contributions.

Think of it this way: it's a pay taxes now (Roth) or pay taxes later (Traditional) scenario. The idea behind the Roth IRA is that you'll likely be in a lower tax bracket now as a young person than you will when you're older. Either way, IRAs are a great tax-sheltered vehicle to save for the future. They do have a lot of other rules you'll want to read up on. So, of course, please refer to the "Resources and Links" section to find out more.

"Why should I put money away when the government already takes money out of my paycheck for Social Security?"

An important question, dear friend. Simply put, your Social Security payments will not be enough to fund your retirement. It's not a good plan to leave your golden years in the hands of other people either (i.e. the government). Social Security has its issues, and if you're at least 40 years old you'll probably get the benefits you're owed. However, there's always a chance the government could decrease your payments if there's mismanagement or if there's more people claiming Social Security benefits than paying into the system (*cough cough Baby Boomers cough cough*).

If you don't want to adjust your lifestyle much in retirement, you're going to have to put money away yourself.

"How much money should I be contributing to my retirement fund?"

A great question from a southern friend! I get this question a lot too. The answer depends on your overall financial situation, and no two situations are the same. First, how much money do you make? Do you have a lot of student loan debt or other types of debt? Do you have an emergency fund? Does your employer match contributions? These are important questions to have answered before deciding how much to invest.

If your company offers a match, you should contribute the necessary amount to receive the match. This is free money. Even if you've got student loans and a car payment, put enough into your retirement account to qualify. Don't leave free money on the table.

Ideally, it would be great if you could afford to contribute up to 15% of your pay into your 401(k) or whatever type of retirement plan in which you participate. Obviously, this isn't feasible for many young people. I would suggest trying to increase your contribution by 1% each year.

If you don't have a retirement plan with your employer, and if you qualify, open a Roth IRA. You can contribute up to $5,500 per year as of 2017. Putting something away is better than doing nothing. Your future self will thank you. Or, if you're feeling really ambitious, contribute to both your 401(k) and a Roth IRA.

"When you're an independent contractor, how can you estimate how much money you'll owe for taxes? How much should I set aside ahead of time to prepare for taxes?"

This question comes from one of my friends in comedy, and is a super common situation among actors, writers, and basically anyone who freelances for a living. If you receive a 1099 instead of a W-2, this is for you:

First, you need to figure out how much money you expect to make and how you're going to file (single, married filing jointly, married filing separately, etc.). From there you'll be able to calculate what tax bracket you're in. Visit the IRS site to see what bracket you fall under. I've included the IRS website in the "Resources and Links" section.

You also need to account for state income taxes in most states. You may need to see if you will owe any county, city, or town taxes as well. Look up your local income taxes. It shouldn't take long with the power of search engines.

Now, you'll have to do some math. Visit the "Resources and Links" section where I've included a website with a cool calculator that'll figure out your federal income tax math for you.

Let's say your federal tax bracket is 15%, and your state tax is 5%. This means that each time you get a paycheck you should save 20% because that's what you'll owe in taxes.

Try to find a savings or money market account with a decent interest rate and stash away your tax money there.

Finally, you've got a couple options for how to pay the taxes. You can either wait until tax time and pay your bill in full, or make estimated quarterly payments throughout the year. I would recommend you make estimated payments. You'll want to pay at least 90% of your estimated tax bill to avoid any penalties for underpayment.

In the "Resources and Links" section you'll find links to the two systems where you can enroll to pay your estimated taxes. The Direct Pay system offered by the IRS is a little easier than the Electronic Federal Tax Payment System.

Thank you to all the friends who sent me questions, I owe you all a round of drinks! Here's to empowering each other through financial literacy.

This essay first appeared on The Funny Financial Planner *blog on March 8, 2017*

How to Tread Water When You're Drowning In Student Loans

Let me start by saying, student loans are the bane of my existence as both a college graduate and a financial planner. I hate them with every fiber of my 5'3" being. I want to talk about student loans probably as much you do. They are about as fun to discuss as politics and religion at your family's Thanksgiving. But please, by all means, continue reading this article because I'm trying my best to make this topic tolerable.

My parents are two hard working middle-class people who wanted nothing more than to send their kids to good schools and watch us soar. They are a product of a different generation; a generation where my dad was able to work through school, and pay for his college degree rather quickly.

Times have changed, and in the past 30 years, the cost of college has risen four times faster than the Consumer Price Index. Four times faster. So the next time a Baby Boomer says, "I worked my way through college, you lazy Millennial!" simply respond with "Shhhh grandpappy, go back to reading *Breitbart*." Working through school is great and necessary, but chances are it won't come close to paying for all the costs of a four-year degree. And in comes our hero: student loans! Hooray! I hope my sarcastic tone is apparent.

If your parents were anything like mine, sending their kids to college was priority *numero uno*. My parents are happily married and both work full-time jobs. Growing up, we were not rich, but we also weren't poverty stricken. My sister and I worked in the summers and I once saved enough money to buy a 1996 Nissan Sentra with subwoofers in the trunk for $500. I miss that purple glorified go-kart every single day. Long story short: We did what we thought we were supposed to do: work hard, study hard, and be good people. My grandparents even gave us savings bonds every holiday and birthday. Yet, somehow I ended up with a trash heap of student loans. So did my little sister. So did most of my cousins and friends.

Our story is the story of millions. I've played the blame game before. Some days I take full responsibility for my naivety in taking out student loans without understanding them. Some days I blame a corrupt system. However, none of this is productive. The fact is we have loans and we must pay them.

So if you are feeling helpless and drowning in the Sea of Sallie Mae, I hope I can provide you a few tips to keep you treading water. Remember, you are only several thousand dollars of the $1.4 trillion in student loan debt...see, that's not so bad!

Get to Know Your Loans

Much like a date you never wanted to be on, you must spend some time getting to know your loans. Getting to know your loans is by far the most important thing you can do before you start repayment. If you learn the ins and outs of your student loans you'll enable yourself to make informed decisions regarding payment plans, consolidation, forgiveness, etc.

So how do you get to know your loans? Do the following:

A. Calculate the total amount you owe. Follow this up with a good cry and screams of despair. Collect yourself and proceed to Step B.

B. Learn about each individual loan including the lender, balance, interest rates, terms, grace period, whether it's federal or private, subsidized or unsubsidized, circumcised or uncircumcised. That last one was just to make sure you're still paying attention.

45

C. Once you have completed Step B, you can begin researching your best repayment options based on the information you've gathered. I know you want me to tell you whether you should consolidate or which loans to pay first, but the truth is it's a case-by-case basis, and financial planners can't make recommendations unless we have all the details about your loans and overall financial situation.

D. Implement a repayment plan that works for you right now. You may have to negotiate with lenders and find out what repayment options you qualify for. As your financial situation improves over time, you'll want to reexamine your repayment plan. The faster you can get rid of these loans the better. Finally, crack a smile each month your loan balance decreases.

Suffer in the Short-Term

We must recognize the difference between what we want and what we need in life. Try to make the hard choices to cut down on your expenses. Throw extra money at your loans when you can. You'll be happy you did in the long run. I'm not saying the sacrifices you make now won't suck, but it's important to live as far below your means as you can while paying down this debt.

Transportation and housing are the two largest monthly expenses. Living with roommates (or mom and dad) and riding your bike to work may be horrible, but it could save you thousands. It's all about short-term sacrifice for long-term gain.

Pro Tip: Don't completely deprive yourself of pleasure when paying down debt. By all means, reward yourself occasionally. Choose your rewards wisely though. Science has shown spending on experiences you'll remember instead of material items will provide you greater happiness.

Don't Ignore Your Loans

You can't pretend they don't exist. There are options for deferring payments, but if you can avoid doing this please do so. If you ignore loans you will have huge problems down the road. Default and delinquency can ruin your credit score and you'll be forced to live with your parents forever. Although, my mom and dad are convinced they are the best roommates on earth. If you are really down on your luck, my folks have a couple of spare bedrooms, a hot tub, and sweet basement. It's not a bad deal if you don't mind my mom walking into your bathroom or bedroom unannounced and my dad singing Sinatra at 5 A.M. while he hammers away on a house project.

Don't Let Loans Consume You

Stop. Take a deep breath. You're going to be okay. I know I just said "don't ignore your loans," but I also don't want you to obsess over them. You still need to live your life. Set up an automatic payment plan, throw extra money at loans when you can, and then go about living your life. Having a good financial plan in place will help you not to panic.

Redefine the American Dream

Who the hell decided the only version of the American Dream is purchasing a house in the suburbs, getting married, and popping out 2.5 kids by your mid-30s? I call bullshit. The American Dream is whatever the hell you want it to be. I have friends who are devastated they cannot yet afford a house, a new car, or a $50,000 wedding. My advice to them is, stop caring! Those are not measures of success. There are more than 40 million Americans with student loan debt. We are all in this together, my friends. Work as hard as you can to pay off the debt, but don't feel like a failure because you haven't "achieved" certain "milestones." Focus on building your skills so you can get that promotion and make more money. Accept that renting an apartment with roommates is not a bad thing, in fact, for most it's a necessity. Stop thinking that purchasing a fancy new car is a hallmark of

47

accomplishment. Instead, when I see someone with a fancy vehicle, I think "Wow, what a shitty financial decision. I hope they know that shiny piece of metal will depreciate by 70% in the next four years. How dumb."

I hope my ranting has inspired you. Student loans are incredibly complicated. I don't have all the answers, but I hope this gives you a metaphorical lifejacket.

This essay first appeared on The Scold *on November 22, 2016*

Five Things You Need to Know About Credit Cards

Credit cards are that friend who influences your bad life decisions, but is always there in your time of need. They are both the devil and angel on your shoulder. As the owner of a credit card, it's essential to remember you are in charge and to not let the sexiness of a line of credit persuade you into bad purchase decisions. Credit cards are nuanced little pieces of plastic.

Here are five things you should know about the plastic in your wallet:

Deferred Interest

This is where the fine print can really come back to bite you in the behind. Many credit cards offer 0% teaser interest rates. How wonderful! What a deal! But wait, there's usually a catch. These 0% introductory rates normally only last so long, usually 3-6 months. When this time expires, whether you're aware of it or not, the interest rate can skyrocket. The new interest rates often exceed 24%, which is insane. If you're carrying a balance at the end of the 0% term, it will be subject to the new extremely high interest rate. If you aren't paying attention, the amount you owe will accumulate quickly. Be extra careful with cards that have deferred interest.

Rewards Programs

Somehow, some way, we are really terrible at using the rewards and points earned on our credit cards. This baffles me because Americans love free stuff. Perhaps, we're simply unaware of the rewards we're earning on our credit cards. Or if you're like me, you just forget you have points. You need to find out what rewards you're entitled to or have earned through your card.

Perhaps another credit card will provide better benefits and incentives. Perhaps your earned points can pay for me to go on vacation with you? I'm just saying, think about it. Don't let those rewards go to waste. Find a card with a reward system you'll actually take advantage of. Really do your homework before opening a new line of credit.

How Your Credit Score is Calculated

Do you know how your credit score is calculated? Did you know there's a formula? I'll break it down for you:

Payment History (35%) - Are you always making payments on time?

Credit Utilization (30%) - This is the aggregate and line-item utilization of your available credit. Basically, how much of your available credit you are using.

Length of Credit History (15%) - The longer your credit history the better.

Types of Accounts in Use (10%) - Auto loans, student loans, mortgages, and credit cards all count. How diversified is your credit?

New Credit (10%) - If you've recently applied for or received new credit.

Your FICO credit score can range from 300-850. Ideally, your credit score will be above 750. Anything under 600 is not good and you should work to improve it.

Interest Rates and Fees

Credit cards charge interest and the rates vary tremendously. You need to know your current interest rate and if it's going to change in the future. If your credit card has an interest rate of 20% and you carry a $1,000 balance throughout the year, you'll end up paying $200 in interest. Yuck. Do your best to pay off your balance each month.

There are also fees associated with credit cards. These can include an annual fee, balance transfer fee, foreign transaction fee, late payment fee, and an over-the-limit fee. Find out which fees your card charges and the corresponding penalty. The more you know, the easier it'll be to avoid costly blunders.

You Have Rights

As a credit card owner you are entitled to certain rights. These rules are made to protect the consumer, so you should be aware of them. Under The Truth in Lending Act, all the issuers' terms of the contract should be written in a way you can understand and contain all information and details. The Fair Credit Billing Act gives you the right to dispute and correct errors without damaging your credit score.

I recommend limited use of credit cards. A good rule of thumb is to not put more on your cards than you can pay off in full each month. Credit card usage requires immense personal discipline. If you don't feel you can be responsible with a credit card, only open one for emergencies and don't keep it in a section of your wallet where you'll be tempted to use it inappropriately. Credit cards are the perpetrator in many a bankruptcy cases. Don't let it happen to you.

This essay first appeared on The Funny Financial Planner *on June 26, 2017*

Surviving the City: A Guide to Living In an Expensive Town

I have several friends in Boston, New York, Los Angeles, and Chicago who all sing the same praises, and shout similar complaints, regarding life in a big city. Most of the positives include the ability to order literally any kind of food to your apartment and the countless number of events, festivals, and hipster-approved activities. The negatives usually involve dirty public transportation, the smell of trash on a hot summer day, and the insane cost of living.

Recent articles suggest that, if you make less than $150,000 in New York, you might as well go live under a bridge. The opportunity to earn a larger salary is far more plentiful in a major metropolitan area, but a city's cost of living severely diminishes the power of your dollar. Six-figures in L.A. is not comparable to six-figures in a rural area.

So what if you want to live in a major city but don't make the big bucks? Do you have to co-op space in a sewer tunnel? Is it possible to live in an expensive urban area on an average salary? Yes, it is possible, but you'll have to compromise, downsize, and prioritize.

Love thy Roommates and Walking

Housing and transportation are our two largest monthly expenses. Cutting down on trips to Starbucks and only ordering well drinks at the bar will save you some cash, but you'll find the most serious opportunities to save in where you live and how you travel.

Do you like roommates? If you live in places such as New York or San Francisco, and don't make a ton of money, I hope your answer is "yes." Living with roommates isn't always easy. I don't have tips on how to find good roommates, because I am the person no one wants to live with. I don't do well with sharing, I like peace and quiet, and I'm beyond awkward in most situations. I could go an entire year without speaking to a roommate for no other reason than I hate one-on-one interactions. I hope you're better than me because roommates can save you thousands over the course of a year.

Secondly, pick a neighborhood to live in that's a solid compromise between price, convenience to work and amenities, and the amount of patience you possess. Think of it this way: how long are you willing to commute to work? How far are you willing to walk to a grocery store, restaurants, etc.? In most cities, the further away from the action, the lower the price. So how much patience are you capable of exuding each day? Your personal happiness could suffer if you don't take this into account.

I love Uber as much as the next girl, but relying on your own car, cabs, or Uber/Lyft is costly. Walk to as many places as possible, utilize public transportation, ride a bike or, better yet, let's make rollerblading cool again. The exception to this is L.A., because you can't go anywhere without a car there (one of ten million reasons I could never live in L.A.).

Meal Prep for Dummies

Sundays aren't just for hangover recovery anymore. Use them to meal prep. You're an adult for Christ's sake. (I write this as I sit un-showered and still in my pajamas at 7 P.M.) The Internet is making it easier to prep food and that's a good thing for people like me. I hate cooking. I suck at it and I don't have a lot of patience and/or skill. The last thing I want to do on a Sunday is meal prep, but every time I do, it saves me time and money the following week. Simply type "meal prep recipes" into the Google machine, and you'll find 3.4 million results. Don't let laziness or a lack of cooking talent stop you in your quest to conserve money. Even though I personally hate meal prepping, it's worth it. I begrudgingly meal prep by turning on my favorite tunes and pretending I'm Giada De Laurentiis who, by the way, has the most adorable tiny T-Rex arms and hands.

Making meals ahead of time is not just healthy for the wallet, lots of muscular people with blogs suggest it's great for your waistline as well.

Track Your Drunken Fun

I can't count the number of times I've woken up after a night out, looked at my bank account and said, "You are an idiot." I suppose it's a rite of passage for young adults. You've got to learn to say "no" to that last round of shots. I know once the drinks get flowing this can be nearly impossible. Even I, as a financial planner well beyond my best partying days, recently slipped up. I was in a bar in Hollywood, I ordered four drinks and the bartender said "that'll be $81." I smiled the most fake of smiles, handed him my debit card, and whispered under my breath, "I hate L.A."

It's crucial to track your fun. Look back at your bank statements from the past few months and figure out just how much of your monthly income is being spent on entertainment. Is there an area that can be improved upon (i.e. examine your spending at restaurants, bars, theaters, strip clubs, cat cafes, etc.)? Even cutting out one night a month in a city could save you a hundred dollars or more.

Downsize, Downsize, Downsize

If you want to live somewhere like New York, you better learn to live without a closet. My first apartment in Boston had one coat closet in each bedroom. We had to get super creative with storing our clothes. Finally, I purged. This experience helped shape me into the minimalist I am today. I like the one-year rule: if you haven't used it in a year then sell it, donate it, or trash it. Selling items you no longer use is a solid way to increase your discretionary income for the month as well.

Downsizing is important in a city because the less stuff you have, the less space you need; and the less space you need, the lower your rent will be. Simple as that. Also, if you plan on moving to New York or downtown Boston, try sleeping in a dog crate for a few nights to get used to the tight quarters these cities provide.

Get A *Legal* Side Hustle

Let me state the obvious here: the best way to improve your quality of life is to make more money. Wow, mind blowing revelation provided by yours truly. Seriously though, use your skills to take advantage of side gigs and opportunities to make a little more dough. Whether you're a talented writer, you've got technical skills, or can sell crafts in an Etsy shop, there are countless ways to pull in extra cash. The Internet has made it possible to get a side gig without leaving our apartments or work 24-7. Did you know people pay to watch women play with their feet via webcam? I'm just saying, there's a lot possibilities when it comes to side hustles.

Pick the Right City

Why do you live in or want to move to this particular city? Have you thought about other cool up-and-coming areas? I'm completely biased when it comes to Boston and New York. I spent close to five years in Boston and I loved every second. New York is my favorite city to visit and I hope to one day have a swanky penthouse there (if I sell enough copies of this book, that's where the royalty checks are going! Just kidding, I still have student loans). But there are other awesome places to move that are cheaper, just as fun, and probably don't have soul-crushing winters. Really do your research before relocating to a pricey city. Write a pros and cons list. Will the additional costs provide you greater personal fulfillment? If yes, then by all means, rent that 100 square foot apartment in Brooklyn.

You don't have to make a million dollars to live in an expensive city, you just have to get creative!

This essay first appeared on The Scold *on December 7, 2016*

When Shit Hits the Fan: Dealing with Death and Divorce

I try my best to be as positive as possible in all aspects of my life. From my personal relationships, to work, to writing, I believe wholeheartedly in the power of positive thinking. So as you can imagine, when I'm asked questions about the financial implications of death and divorce it can be quite a challenge to put a positive spin on it. I may be annoyingly optimistic, but I understand life sucks sometimes. No one is immune to personal hardship. Do I want to talk to you about preparing financially for death and divorce? Ummm no. I really don't. But I'm going to, because we need to accept the fact that these things happen. If you're lucky, you won't ever deal with divorce. If you're really lucky, you'll also live to be 100 and die peacefully in your sleep with millions left for your heirs.

The following tips are about providing yourself, and your family, with peace of mind and not becoming a posthumous financial burden. I've thought a lot about how to address death and divorce with empathy, honesty, and humor with clients. It's not easy, but we all need to hear it.

What Happens When I Die?

I don't know where we go when we die. I hope heaven is Fenway Park on a warm June day. Ideally, I'll have access to unlimited pizza from Regina's and cold Sam Adams Summer Ale (sorry for being a stereotypical Masshole).

Unfortunately, I do know what happens to families when a loved one passes away and a will isn't there to divvy up assets. Or what happens when family has to scrape enough money together to afford a funeral. It makes the grieving process even more terrible.

You Need a Will

For a few hundred dollars (usually) you can legally decide how you want your assets distributed, who gets what, and who is responsible for carrying out your wishes. I can't tell you how important this is. When you die without a will, how your assets are distributed (bank accounts, retirement accounts, real estate, etc.) is dependent upon the state in which you live. Usually the laws favor the spouse or domestic partner.

With a will, you get to decide exactly how you want your most valuable assets to be inherited. Why leave what you worked your whole life for in the hands of the state? This is also where a lot of stress and contention can happen among family members. Your family is already grieving, why make it worse?

Also, you can make it clear in your will if you'd rather be buried, cremated, or cryogenically frozen for science (*raises hand*). After I'm cryogenically frozen, I'd like my family to throw a massive kegger with a live band in celebration of my whimsical life. It would be preferable if Oprah, Tina Fey, and any available members of the New England Patriots could attend. Mark this as my first feeble attempt to lighten up this very dark essay.

Have an Honest Discussion

We all know communication is key to any solid relationship. If you have specific wishes in dying and death, you can't expect your family to know unless you discuss it with them. Some other points to consider discussing with your closest relatives include: how will funeral expenses be paid for? Is there a will? Who is inheriting what, and is it specified in the will? Other than discussing sex with my parents, I cannot think of a conversation I'd want to have less. Alas, we all know the importance of a parent explaining the birds and the bees. This is no different.

Dying Isn't Cheap

The average cost of a funeral in the United States in 2016 was closing in on $7,200. That's outrageous. Because $7,200 isn't exactly chump change, it's going to be

important that your spouse or kids know ahead of time how funeral expenses are to be paid.

Keep Beneficiary Info Up-To-Date

Your bank, retirement, and brokerage accounts likely all have the option to name specific beneficiaries (the person or people who will directly inherit those assets should you pass away). The beneficiary information needs to be accurate and up-to- date in order to avoid a legal-shmegal mess. Also, let's make sure your will and beneficiaries are consistent. Named beneficiaries override the will, by the way.

Let's move on to something less morbid. Divorce!

If you are about to file for divorce, or are in the middle of a divorce, here are some tips:

Be Organized

You really need to know what is yours, what is your spouse's, and what is jointly owned as far as your assets go. Get your financial documents gathered and organized in case there are any questions regarding assets and liabilities during divorce proceedings. Be in the know! The more you understand about your financial situation and how it'll change, the less overwhelmed you'll feel during this transition.

Know Your Credit Score

Take a look at your credit score during and after your divorce. Make sure any disputes are resolved and your ex isn't using joint credit cards you're trying to dissolve. You can get a free credit report from one of the three major credit reporting agencies: Equifax, Experian, and TransUnion.

Get a P.O. Box

This one is about protecting yourself and your privacy. You'll probably receive correspondence from attorneys and other professionals throughout the course of your divorce. A P.O. Box will help ensure you actually receive important messages and documents, and that you're the only eyes reading them.

Save, Save, Save

Divorce is freaking expensive. If you know you're heading for Splitsville, start putting away money now. You'll owe legal and other professional fees, but you'll also be on your own paying for everyday living expenses. Help ease the blow by putting money away ahead of time.

Change Your Beneficiaries/Will/Medical Directives

You're probably not going to want your ex-husband/wife to be the recipient of all your accounts anymore, so you're going to need to update your beneficiaries, will, and any medical directives you have in place. Ugh tedious, I know.

Get Your Own Accounts

If you're divorcing, you're also going to want to open your own checking and savings accounts, as well as a credit card in your own name.

Prepare to Downsize and Cut Expenses

This might be one of the rougher parts of your divorce transition. You'll be providing for yourself now and you'll likely have to adjust your expenses. Unfortunately, downsizing and learning to live within your new means is a harsh reality for divorcées. If you're unsure how to make financial adjustments, there are financial planners who specialize in helping people transition after divorce.

Death and divorce are two of the most painful events life can throw at you. While we hope our experiences with both are minimal, if you are prepared financially, the transition to the next chapter in your life will be a bit smoother.

This essay first appeared on The Scold *on January 17, 2017*

Invest Like the Badass You Are

Listen up! I'm pissed and I'm about to give you a fiery speech. I just Googled "Top Celebrity Investors" for literally no reason at all, and all the lists I came across had one, maybe two, female celebs on them. This is both infuriating and saddening. Shout out to Tyra Banks for landing on many of these lists. She is savvy as fuck. I feel like she's my new kindred spirit, you know, because of our supermodel looks and business acumen. Side note: I actually laughed out loud writing that last sentence.

Back to my fiery rant: ladies, we need to get into the investing game. Nothing is stopping us, except ourselves. Now is the time for action. Trust me, I've heard every excuse in the book for not investing. So let me give you a few reasons you should:

So You Can Not Be a Pauper in Your Old Age

First and foremost, you need to invest (at a minimum in an employer-sponsored retirement plan or IRA) so that when you become a vivacious cougar, you'll actually be able to maintain your quality of life. It's frightening how many older Americans are forced to live in poverty or become dependent on younger relatives because they didn't save enough for retirement. The ramifications of not having enough in your golden years are tremendously painful.

So You Won't Be a Burden on Your Children/Relatives

This is all about growing old with dignity and grace. Yes, we should absolutely take care of our parents and grandparents. But, real talk, taking care of elderly relatives is a huge financial and emotional burden for the caretakers. I love my parents, and I'd do anything for them, but I really hope they retire with enough cash to hire someone to provide sponge baths if and when that time comes. (I bet you $10 my mom read this paragraph and audibly muttered, "Jesus Christ,

Catie, what's wrong with you?" Which is also a question my family asks at least once per week.) I know I don't want to be a burden on anyone, and I'm sure you don't either.

Women Live a Long Ass Time

The risk of living longer than you expected is high, which means you could potentially outlive your money. With advances in medicine and technology, we're all going to be bionic and drugged to the gills. We're going to live forever, unless the rising seawater consumes us first. This is to be determined. You'll need more money than you think to last into your eighth, ninth, and tenth decades. Personally, I hope to be raising hell in my old age. There's nothing better than a sassy octogenarian.

You'll Learn A Lot and That's Empowering

I know people think personal finance is boring, but honestly it's not. Investing is so interesting once you give it a chance. When I learn something new about money I get a surge of energy and confidence. Also, Sheryl Sandberg wants us to *Lean In* and I don't disobey Sheryl Sandberg orders.

So You Can Impress People at Parties

Your investing intellect is a great icebreaker at social events. You'll be the life of the party! Start throwing out financial industry jargon with reckless abandon and people will be drawn to you like bees to honey. I haven't been invited to a party in five years.

Now let's chat about the main reasons women don't invest:

You're Scared

You don't want to lose money. You don't want to make a bad investment. You don't want to get screwed over. I get it. These are rational fears, and there is risk to investing. The important thing is to know how much risk you're able to withstand. The best advice I can give is to stop freaking out about the news. The worst thing you can do is react to every bad thing you read or see on television. The stock market goes up and down every single day. If you make money decisions based on fear and emotion, you will lose every time.

You Don't Know What You're Doing

Everyone has to start somewhere. This is, again, all about educating yourself. You will never have all the answers, but it's not as hard you might think to gain a basic understanding of investing. There are tons of resources out there. There are people like me who have good intentions and want to teach you as well. There's no shame in asking for help.

You Don't Know Who to Trust

This is an extremely valid fear. There are some scummy people in the financial world. Trust your gut. If a financial professional seems sketchy, they probably are. If they're honest and transparent about their fees and investing philosophy, then that's a good sign. There are a lot of great financial planners out there (I personally know many of them). There are also planners who work within specific niches. Get on the Internet and find one that may be able to cater to your specific needs.

How Do We Get Started?

I'm not going to give you any "hot stock tips," those are only for suckers. I'm not going to tell you what your investment portfolio should look like either (everybody's risk tolerance and needs are different). I am, however, going to tell you that investing is imperative to ensure you'll have enough money for the rest of your life.

Develop a Long-Term Strategy

Investing is a marathon not a sprint. The best way to make

money through investing is via a long-term strategy. Long-term in this case means many years. You aren't going to make money overnight. It takes a long ass time to accumulate wealth through investing and the earlier you can start the better. That's right, I'm talking to you people in your early twenties. Start as soon as you freaking can. Once you invest your money, just let it be. Reviewing it annually is great, but don't get tempted to buy and sell all the time. Trading fees, short and long-term capital gains taxes, and bad investment decisions can quickly eat away at your earnings. It's a losing strategy and a glorified form of gambling. You won't consistently win. I could get into the tax consequences of buying and selling your investments, but I'm not trying to give you a migraine right now.

Patience Isn't Just a Virtue, It's Required

If you're going to be the Tyra Banks of investing, you're going to need a lot of patience. Resisting the constant noise coming from the media, the ridiculous tips you'll hear from family members, and the temptation to invest with emotion instead of sticking to your strategy will require immense patience. Warren Buffett famously said "The stock market has a very efficient way of transferring wealth from the impatient to the patient."

You're Not a Goddamn Fortune Teller

Without getting too technical, I generally urge clients to take a passive approach to investing. This usually means investing in a mix of index funds and exchange traded funds (ETFs) that track the overall movement of the markets. An index fund is a type of investment portfolio, similar to a mutual fund, that's designed to track a component of a market index (think S&P 500). It's goal is to provide the investor wide market exposure for a low cost. Normally, if you wanted to invest in all the companies in the S&P 500, it would cost you a lot of fucking money. An index fund makes investing, for example, in all the S&P 500 companies affordable. ETFs are similar to index funds, but they are bought and sold like regular stocks. They have lower fees than mutual funds and are considered more liquid (you can convert them to cash fairly quickly). Why do I encourage most people to stick with index funds and ETFs? Because I'm not a fortuneteller, you aren't a fortuneteller, and those annoying talking heads on CNBC are not fortunetellers. A passive long-term approach to investing seeks to eliminate making choices based on what you think might happen. Making money decisions based on speculation is the same as gambling and baby, I've already burned too many bridges in Vegas.

It's Not Too Late, but It's Never Too Early

We get this excuse a lot in my financial planning practice: "I'm too old to start" or "It's too late for me." No! Stop it right now, Debbie Downer! It's important to know it's not too late to invest for your future. In the same sense, you can avoid becoming this person by starting your retirement savings now as a young professional.

You will be a better investor than all of your friends by simply getting together a game plan, creating a well-diversified portfolio of passive investments, and exhibiting some damn patience. I hope you now feel as confident as Tyra Banks walking a Victoria's Secret runway.

This essay first appeared on The Scold *November 16, 2016*

Why You Need Multiple Income Streams

Creating multiple income streams is the ticket to achieving all your financial goals. Multiple streams of income is defined as money coming in from more than one job or investment. The wealthiest people on the planet have dozens, if not hundreds, of income streams. The average millionaire has seven sources of income. So it begs the question: how does one build multiple income streams when you're already working like a dog at your full-time job? It's really not as difficult as you think.

There are two types of income: active and passive. Active income is money earned through material participation and services you've provided. Active income includes your primary salary and if you work any other side gigs like waitressing, sales, mowing your neighbor's lawn, and things of that nature. Passive income includes interest received, dividends, capital gains, rental income, advertising income, royalties, etc. Basically, passive income is earned through vehicles where you are not materially participating.

If you're interested in increasing your number of income streams and overall take-home pay, it'll require some time and effort up front, but it can be done. Here are some of my favorite alternative streams of income:

Sell Your Stuff - Start an Etsy store. Creativity and craftiness goes a long way on the Internet. Etsy is a terrific place to set up a virtual shop to sell your arts and crafts. If you're not the creative type, but need to unload some clothes, household goods, or unused stuff lying around the house, create an EBay sellers account. One man's trash is another's treasure, am I right?

Invest - Of course I'm going to tell you to create an investment portfolio. The dividend and interest received from a well- diversified portfolio can create an income stream for you now as well as later. Be sure to know your risk tolerance, time- horizon, and what investments are best suited for you before moving any money.

Freelance - If you like to write, design, or have any skills suitable for a freelance market, there's money to be made. The life of a freelancer is not always easy, but if you keep your eyes and ears open for opportunities, or perhaps even create your own opportunities, freelancing is a great way to burn some creative energy while earning cash on the side.

Blog/Affiliate Marketing - If you run a blog, a website, or have a considerable social media following (particularly Instagram) you may want to look into advertising and affiliate marketing. AdSense by Google is a way to allow, and get paid for, advertisements on your website or blog. You won't get rich overnight through AdSense, but if you get enough page views, it'll put extra cash in your pocket. Affiliate marketing is when you recommend or promote a product or service. You'll be paid a commission from each sale that's generated by you. Instagram, podcasts, and blogs are currently the Meccas of affiliate marketing.

Real Estate - Buying a home to either flip and resell, or rent to tenants, is a common investment-based income stream. Real estate is a tricky business though, so you'd really have to do your homework before jumping in. If you're interested in real estate, it's best to find a mentor who's successful in the business and begin working with them.

Royalties - For musicians and writers, there's no sweeter sound than the words "royalty check." The easiest way to earn royalty checks is by writing an e-book and selling it online. You likely won't earn life changing money through self-published e-books, but if you've got a great story or something to teach, an e-book is a terrific way to boost your bank account.

Create an Online Class - This is an interesting concept that was recently brought to my attention. Many people who have expertise in certain areas are creating online classes to teach people around the world their particular skill. There are companies on the Internet who will help you host these classes, and I believe this is going to be a big part of the future of online education.

Work a Side Hustle - Ah, yes, the good old second job. The income streams I've mentioned above are all either forms of passive income or online income. If none of those are up your alley, then we've still got restaurants and bars that need help, children who need babysitters, dogs who need walking, and lawns that need mowing. Ain't no shame in your hustle game.

Whether you choose passive income streams or active income streams to build your wealth, it's going to require a bit of commitment on your part. You have to do the research, put in the time and effort, and stay dedicated in order to build effective multiple streams of income. It's a good thing you're already brilliant and resourceful. Now go get 'em.

This essay first appeared on The Funny Financial Planner *blog on July 14, 2017*

Building Wealth is Easy (Or at Least It Should Be)

Building wealth is easy. Sounds like a scam right? Well, maybe building wealth isn't easy, but there is a simple formula. When executed with discipline and determination, the formula will lead to wealth over the long-term. Learning how to become wealthy isn't difficult. It's the implementation of the plan and patience to see it through that's hard.

What do you need to do to be wealthy?

Make as Much Money as Possible

You're probably saying, "Thank you, for stating the obvious you heartless she-devil." I know, I know. Hear me out, though. Building wealth starts with the income we have coming in each month. Whatever you do professionally, try to maximize your earning potential as quickly as you can. Obviously, the more money we have coming in, the more effectively we can save and invest. It all starts with income.

A well-paying job begins with finding the right industry, making yourself as valuable as possible to the company, and living well below your means. If you're a blogger who earns next to nothing, like me, educating yourself on how to best monetize your profession is crucial. There are many wonderful occupations that, unfortunately, don't pay great salaries. If you work in a lower-paying industry, the road will be tougher, but not impossible. Always look for chances to maximize your pay. Sometimes this means picking up side hustles.

This is just the tip of the iceberg, of course. Negotiating for salary and benefits will play an integral part in your journey. Earning the proper credentials and education is also necessary. Finally, living a lifestyle that isn't focused on keeping up with the Joneses is by far the most important step. As we earn more money in our career, we tend to suffer from "lifestyle creep." This is when our expenses slowly climb along with our additional income. Avoiding lifestyle creep will help you achieve your financial goals. Just because you're making more money, doesn't necessarily mean you need to be spending more money.

Save Your Cash

You need to save enough money so when your appliances need repair, your car dies, or some unforeseen emergency arises, it won't derail your financial future.

Generally, financial planners recommend an emergency fund that's able to cover six months of living expenses. Most people can't save this amount overnight, so set a goal as to how much you'll put in your emergency fund each month. Remember, it's most effective if you automate your savings. Slowly but surely you'll get there. If you happen to experience an emergency during your saving period, you'll be glad you at least have something to lessen the blow.

Once you've got your emergency fund in place, it's important to save for other goals such as vacations, retirement, and education. It's preferable to save for these objectives in separate accounts.

Setting goals in advance, giving each earned dollar a job, and automating your savings is the best strategy to make certain you've got enough put away for the future.

Invest Wisely

Letting your money sit in cash is a waste. Yes, it's important to have cash as part of your overall financial picture, but letting too much of it sit on the sidelines is detrimental. Cash barely keeps pace with inflation, so it could be losing value instead of gaining. You need to invest, and learning how to be a decent investor is not as difficult as you think. We covered this in an earlier essay, but start with your employer's retirement plan. Make sure you're contributing enough to receive any available match. Never turn down free money.

Outside of your employer's retirement plan you can open other investment accounts as well. Most people tend to opt for Traditional or Roth IRAs. The advantageous tax properties of these accounts will help your money grow faster over time compared to taxable accounts.

Whether you're investing in your 401(k), IRA, or taxable investment account, be sure the investments you choose are properly diversified. This can usually be accomplished using a mix of low-cost index funds and ETFs.

As always, education is key. There are many valuable resources online to learn the basic tenets of investing. Be accountable to your future by reading about personal finance and investing even after you've completed this book. You won't regret it.

Be Patient

Wealth takes a long time to build. This is a marathon and you'll be much happier if you start the race as a young person with fresh legs. The stock market is going to go up and down. You're going to hear a bunch of terrible advice as to what to do with your money. You'll be tempted to spend on luxuries and participate in wasteful consumption. Stay the course. Pay the fear mongers, talking heads, and naysayers no mind. If you continue to live far below your means, save diligently for goals, and invest for the long-term, you will build wealth. How much wealth you're able to accrue depends on these factors as well as the amount of time you let your plan play out. Wealth isn't built overnight. See, wasn't that easy?

This article first appeared on The Funny Financial Planner *blog on February 24, 2017*

A Word on Intersectionality, Rigged Systems, and Financial Advice

Do you ever feel like "the system" is rigged against you? The system can be many things. For me it was the student loan industry. I felt they preyed upon my family and took advantage of us for wanting to live our American Dream of going to college. Our status as blue-collar people in a low-income town made us vulnerable to exploitative lenders looking to increase profits on the backs of unassuming people simply trying to make better lives for themselves. The injustice I felt during that time is relatively mild compared to the way financial institutions, businesses, and even government agencies often target and/or discriminate against marginalized communities; particularly people of color, low-income families, the LGBTQ+ community, and women.

I've spent the past few years discussing how you can improve your own financial life through my writing and I hope you've learned a few lessons. At a minimum, I hope I've made you smile and given you a little bit of hope. What we haven't really addressed are the institutional issues that continually hurt marginalized groups. What I'm talking about today is how much more difficult it is to become financially independent if you are not white, not male, and not heterosexual. Let's not pretend discrimination doesn't exist.

Lately, I've heard a lot of people saying something to the effect of "your advice is good, but it's not always applicable to everyone." This is true. I mainly talk about money from the perspective of a middle-class white woman in the suburbs. Unfortunately, some of the advice I give isn't always intersectional.

So I wanted to take a second to address that.

I need to do a better job. My industry needs to do a better

73

job. Our society needs to understand we're not all on equal footing when we set out on the path to financial freedom. Financial freedom is not as easily achieved if you are discriminated against; or raised in a low-income community where education is underfunded; or turned away from jobs because of the way you look, or who you love. These are very real issues that impede the path to financial success for millions of people.

Oh, I cannot wait for the "well, actually..." crowd to come at me for this one. Here's the thing: we all need to be personally accountable for our financial lives, but we can't ignore the greater institutionalized issues within our society like predatory student loan and housing lenders, shifty credit card issuers, the small group of billionaires and millionaires essentially running our political system, the lack of funding for education in low- income communities, and the utter disdain for women within the highest ranks of business and government. This all goes hand-in-hand with the classism, racism, sexism, and every -ism and -phobia plaguing our institutions and culture. While we all must do what we can to help ourselves, we can't ignore the fact marginalized communities are operating within a system that often treats them unfairly.

I will never believe hope is lost. I believe we can collectively push the needle forward on social issues, despite the difficult odds. I would love to see a world where every person has the same opportunity to reach financial independence. Until that time, we must advocate for the less fortunate.

So how do we do that?

Financial Literacy

For my fellow financial planners and educators, we need to go teach financial literacy in underserved places. Schools, community centers, shelters, libraries, wherever you go there are people who need these skills. Let's do our part.

Continue to Educate Yourself

We are nothing without knowledge. I don't care how "woke" you think you are, don't stop reading and learning from the perspectives of those who don't look or live like you. My grandmother once told me, "Be smart enough to know you don't know anything at all." This piece of advice has stuck with me. I can't begin to know the struggles of many marginalized communities, but it is my responsibility as a human functioning within this society to learn. Then, I must take that knowledge and use it to help improve those problems. This is our duty as compassionate human beings. You don't have to solve world hunger, but at least have enough heart to acknowledge the problem, and go feed a kid or two.

Vote

Fucking vote for candidates who actually have your best interest at heart. Gone are the days of complacency and not informing yourself about candidates for federal, state, and local elections. We all have a civic responsibility and, if you like living in a democratic republic in which you are free to write shit on the Internet and go to brunch on Sundays, I suggest you start engaging in the political process.

Run for Office

Let's be real. We need better people in government. These shitbag politicians often rise through the ranks completely unopposed. You want to see your values reflected throughout society? Then run for office, vote for people who share your views, and continue to raise awareness.

Don't shut up. When we see inequality and injustice, we are complicit if we say nothing. Be brave and stand up for those who are treated unfairly. Keep raising the issue until it is solved. Don't call yourself an ally, a feminist, or an advocate if real and consistent action doesn't follow your words. Martin Luther King, Jr. said it best: "In the End, we will remember not the words of our enemies, but the silence of our friends."

Start Listening

We all need to be better listeners. Americans love to impose their views on others while simultaneously existing in their sanctimonious echo chambers. We don't listen to opposing views, we don't try to understand the struggles of our peers. We listen only to formulate a response. We need to start listening to understand. This isn't easy. I'm the first to admit I suck at listening, but I'm willing to try harder and keep my opinionated mouth shut while someone else is talking.

Ask Questions

If you don't understand certain communities, opposing views, or why someone would choose to put pineapple on a pizza, ask questions! Don't ask condescendingly or rhetorically, either. Ask questions honestly and earnestly. Ask open-ended questions that'll encourage civil discourse. Ask with a heart and head that's ready to hear answers that might not be pleasant to one's ears. Also, remember, there's a time and a place to play devil's advocate, but know that in doing so, people will want to throw you off a bridge.

Support Institutions That Support You

In the financial world, I'm talking about the Consumer Finance Protection Bureau. This bureau is not perfect, but it was put into place to protect average everyday people from companies trying to take advantage of you. Support the fiduciary rule too. The fiduciary rule is when a financial advisor or planner is legally obligated to act in your best interest. This is a good rule that aims to keep financial professionals honest and putting your hard-earned money to the best use possible. Don't let political nonsense distract you from protections that are actually good for you. Our society will continue to evolve, but don't for one second think you are insignificant and can't help enact change. Don't take the easy way out. Be a productive and compassionate citizen. I know it's overwhelming and big issues seem out of our hands, but that's the attitude that got a reality TV star elected as president and it's no longer acceptable. We have to do better for ourselves, and for the most vulnerable among us. Right now, for many people, the system seems rigged against them. These are fixable problems if we take the necessary actions together.

Clearly, I'm not just talking about inequalities in the financial systems now. Sorry about that, but I'm feeling feisty today. I know it sounds like I'm on a high horse or preaching from a soapbox, but you should know these are all things I've had to say to myself in the past year. I'm not any better than anyone else. I don't have all the answers, but I don't think we should ever stop searching for the solutions to these big problems.

This essay first appeared on The Scold *on July 11, 2017*

Part II: Essays on Career

The word "career" scares me. It's so much more than a job. It implies permanence. A career is something everyone wants to be proud of. Your career encompasses all your professional achievements. We spend so much of our young adulthood frantically trying to advance our professional status, but did you know the average American changes careers three to four times? I'm not talking about jobs, I'm telling you full on career changes. So just because you don't love your career right now doesn't mean you're stuck forever.

The career section of this book is dedicated to helping you navigate the confusing professional world. The path to a fulfilling career is defined by its winding turns and numerous obstacles. At times you may find yourself turning around to get back on track. At other points, you'll take huge leaps toward the summit. Don't expect this to be a smooth and linear journey. We will work nearly 100,000 hours in our lifetime. How much value and fulfillment you get from each of those hours will depend on your ability to learn the lessons and enjoy the ride.

I didn't have a clue what I wanted to do with my life until I was 28. I wavered between industries and specialties, and I was never truly happy with the job I was in. I was immature, but I also knew I hadn't found my purpose and where I was truly valuable. Even today, I'm still adjusting and changing my professional dreams.

It's okay not to know what you want to do, or to change your idea of a "dream job" every decade. We're humans whose interests, skills, and values are evolving along with our increasingly fat asses. It often feels like our friends are surpassing us and we're the only one without a definitive life plan. If you feel like you're the only one still "figuring it out" just remember Colonel Sanders didn't start Kentucky Fried Chicken until he was 63 years old. Anyone who tells you they know exactly what they're doing in their career is probably full of shit, too.

My point is that you have more time than you think. If you work hard and use every challenge and opportunity as a chance to better yourself, your career progression will naturally bring you overall satisfaction.

Nailing the Interview

If you've reached the point in the job application process where a hiring manager invites you to participate in either a phone or in-person interview, pat yourself on the back, because you've already outlasted dozens, maybe hundreds, maybe thousands of other candidates. This is the final stage, and you need to impress the pants off the interviewer (not literally). So, how exactly do you show them the best possible version of you?

After getting turned down for an embarrassing number of jobs in my twenties, I've compiled a list of things I've learned to nail your next interview. Please feel free to learn from my errors, and maybe you'll save yourself from a little humiliation and soul-crushing rejection.

Be Yourself

Hiring managers are trained to see through bullshit. Be confident enough to be yourself. You are great, you are unique, and there is only one of you in the world. Of course you should be humble and gracious, but don't downplay your abilities and accomplishments. Never apologize for who you are and the great things you've done.

Research the Company

Do you want to hear a horror story? I once had two job interviews in one week. I was also working full-time for another company. I was stressed out and eager to make a good impression. I extensively researched both companies with whom I was interviewing. During the first interview, the hiring manager said, "So, tell me what you know about our company." I began spouting facts and figures with conviction. The interviewer's face turned confused and red. It was in that awkward moment I realized I was telling him facts about the other company I was going to interview with a few days later. Needless to say, I didn't recover from that egregious error and was not offered a job. I've also never told anyone that story because it is humiliating and I was so fucking mad at myself. It took me a long time to get over that gaff. So, in conclusion, the lesson here is try not to fuck up your interview. Or if you have multiple interviews, schedule them far enough apart so that you won't get confused.

Are you feeling any secondhand embarrassment after reading about my idiocy? Would you like to hear one more interview story? This one is about my dad. Several years ago my dad was conducting interviews for his department. He began questioning the young candidate sitting in front of him, and in a display of his "boss" status, placed his arms behind his head and leaned back in his fancy bossman chair. He leaned too far back. He flipped over. Ass over teakettle. The young man was not offered the job. Can you imagine that guy going back to his family and telling them, "I don't think I'm getting that job. The hiring manager probably never wants to see my face again." The moral of this story is the person interviewing you is probably a little nervous and wants to make a good impression as much as you do. They're representing their company after all. We're also all humans and shit happens. If you aren't hired for a certain position, it might not have been something you did. Maybe you weren't a good fit, maybe they decided to promote from within, or maybe the interviewer flipped over in his chair. That's just life. Learn what lessons you can and quickly move on.

Well now that I've gone off on a tangent, let's get back on track! You must do your research before heading into an interview. What's the company's mission? Who are their competitors? How long has the company been around? What's the culture like? This is information to arm yourself with before walking into a hiring manager's office. Also, should you receive a job offer, you're going to want to know important things like the financial health of the company, especially if it's a start up, and what the media is saying about the business. The more you know about your potential employer, the more prepared you'll be in the interview. Plus, you'll be able to make a well-informed decision if you're offered the job.

Have Questions Prepared

At the end of every interview they'll ask the standard, "So, do you have any questions?" If you say no, you'll give off a disinterested and underprepared vibe. Come ready with questions that'll reveal your interest in the company and show you've done some level of research. It's recommended you have two to three questions prepared. Here are a few examples of good questions to ask during an interview:
1. What are your short-term and long-term expectations for a person in this role?
2. What qualities are needed for someone to excel in this role?
3. What do you like best about working for this company?
4. What are the next steps in the interview process?
5. What are the biggest opportunities and challenges facing the company and this department?

Here are a few examples of bad questions to ask during an interview:
1. What's your policy on inter-office hookups?
2. What time does everyone usually head to happy hour?
3. How often do you drug test?
4. Will my office be next to that dime piece? *points to attractive person walking by*
5. Are you single/pregnant/sick? (Don't be an idiot. Keep it professional.)

Send a Handwritten Thank-You Note

This is old school, but I don't know anyone on Earth who

doesn't love receiving a handwritten thank-you note. It's courteous and shows you care. Take the time to do it. Mail it within a day of interviewing so you'll stay top of mind. Honestly, I don't care how fast technology progresses; a handwritten note never goes out of style.

When you walk into your interview prepared, you'll be more confident and at ease. Do some meditation or yoga before you go to your interview, eat a healthy meal, and make sure your energy is up. If you're like me and have a sensitive stomach, you'll want to eat a couple Tums or take some Pepto-Bismol about an hour before sitting down with the hiring manager. I wish I was kidding.

Things Not to Put On Your Resume

Depending on your industry, the format of your resume or CV will vary. It doesn't matter if you're an actor, writer, engineer, accountant, or garbageman, if your resume looks like crap you're putting yourself at a severe disadvantage. First, let's talk about what not to put on your resume:

Irrelevant Experience

Don't feel like you have to put every single job you've ever worked since you were 15 years old on your resume. Irrelevant experience is just clutter and a hiring manager will see right through it. Only include irrelevant experience if you can explain how the skills and experience gained in that job will assist you in the position for which you are now applying.

Your Hobbies

I'm really sorry, but no one gives a flying fuck what you do in your spare time. Your scrapbooking obsession or passion for CrossFit does not belong on a resume.

Lies

Don't lie on your resume. It will come back to bite you in the ass and can have serious repercussions on your career. The tone of your resume should reflect how your experience and skills will be of value to the company and role for which you have applied. You can word things carefully and craftily, but don't exaggerate, and for the love of Beyoncé, do not lie. This seems like a given, but a good hiring manager can smell a bullshitter from a mile away. Even worse, you don't want to get called out for lying and risk getting blacklisted in your industry.

Anything That Describes Your Looks

Unless you're in the entertainment industry, describing the way you look shouldn't appear anywhere on your resume. It's

inappropriate and definitely not legal for an employer to hire someone based on physical appearance.

Things That Make You Look Insane

This could be a variety of things. Don't write outrageous statements. Don't use an email address that makes you sound like a pre-teen. Don't mention you've watched Star Wars 253 times. Don't mention that you think astrology is a reliable career-placement tool. It's not. These are all real life examples that cost real people real jobs.

Poor Grammar and Spelling

In the age of autocorrect and spellcheck, there is no reason for your resume to contain grammatical or spelling errors. Find yourself a trustworthy proofreader. It's very difficult to self- edit, and you will be judged for poor spelling and grammar. Mistakes display carelessness and are completely preventable. It's important to have a second or third set of eyes check your work, just to be safe.

What should you include on your resume?

Your Contact Information

Um, yes, hi, hello, don't be a ding-dong and forget to put your contact information on your resume. Contact information includes your name, phone number, and email. Do not, I repeat, do not include a link to your Tinder profile. I don't care how attractive you find the hiring manager.

Your Relevant Experience

The interviewer needs to know if you are qualified for this job. Your past work experience should detail your responsibilities and outline your skills. If you're still young and lacking experience, figure out how your internships, summer jobs, and part-time work helped you build the necessary qualifications.

Your Education

C's get degrees, y'all. Go ahead and put that bachelor's degree on your resume with pride. Also, any other relevant education should be included as well, such as certificates, training programs, and other coursework. It's best if you list your highest level of education first. You'd rather the hiring manager notice your master's degree before your high school diploma, right? If you're a recent college graduate, you can include your GPA, but after a certain period of time, GPA doesn't matter as much.

Keywords

We live in a world where a form of technology will likely read your resume before a human. In order to pass the robot test, your resume should include keywords that will green-light you to the next round. The keywords should relate to the specific job and highlight the skills, qualities, and credentials the company is looking for in this position. If you are unsure what keywords to include in your resume, take a look at the job posting online and the company website itself. The language the company uses to describe the particular role and the overall business will clue you in on words to use on your resume. It's recommended you use keywords in your cover letter as well.

Highlight Accomplishments and Achievements, Quantify Where Applicable

In addition to your experience and skills, it's important for a hiring manager to see what you've achieved. Your accomplishments should highlight the challenges you've faced, the actions you took, and the results you attained. Use statistics where you can, because numerical proof of your impact is a great way to stand out. Finally, don't forget to include any promotions you've received.

Have Integrity

Your integrity and professional reputation is invaluable. Once it's damaged, it'll be incredibly hard to rebuild. This begins with your resume.

Girl, Get Yourself a Raise!

I was scrolling Instagram, as I normally do at 3 A.M. when I can't sleep and am thinking about every mistake I've ever made, when I noticed an account I follow called "Betches" was promoting "National Ask for a Raise Month." My first thought was "Mother of God please let me fall back asleep," followed by, "Ask for a Raise Month? Hell yeah, I can get on board with that!"

I know I've got some dudes reading this, and by all means I hope you take these tips and apply them to your own careers, but I really want to take this opportunity to address my fellow Queens, Kweens, Lady Bosses, Bad Bitches, Nasty Women, and Beyoncés. We need to do our part to close the wage gap. This means we're going to have to put our big girl pantsuits on and ask for what we deserve. This means no more apologizing for being bold. Don't allow yourself to be interrupted. You determine your value and, I'm telling you that value should be limitless.

To improve your financial situation you can go one of two ways. You either decrease expenses or increase income. I'm guessing we all prefer the latter. So, if you're going to stay at your current company, how do you make more money? You ask for a raise! If you're a woman you're probably already making 20% less than your male peers, so why not at least try to pull even? Wait, no, scratch that. Get the money you freaking deserve. If you deserve more than your peers, then you damn well better ask for it.

How do you ask and ultimately receive the raise you deserve? Well, it takes some prep on your part. No one is going to willingly approach you and hand you money, unless you're Oprah or an exotic dancer.

Step 1: Prepare Your Case

You better have some terrific reasons to back up your case for a raise. Ask yourself the following questions: Why do you deserve a raise? What have you done that's added value to the company? What projects did you complete or lead? How have you displayed leadership and initiative? What are your goals

within the company? How have you challenged yourself within your current role?

Write these answers down, know them by heart, and present them to your boss when they inevitably ask a form of the question: "So why do you think you deserve a raise?"

Step 2: Know Your Worth

What are people with your title, responsibilities, and experience earning at your company as well as at other companies? Come prepared with some evidence as to why you deserve as much, or more, than people with comparable duties. Glassdoor.com and salary.com are not bad places to start. It's crucial to go into your meeting knowing exactly what you want for a salary and benefits. The more specific you are, the better. If you find yourself in a negotiating position, know what your goal is and what your limits are. Don't be afraid to communicate these items either.

Step 3: Practice, Practice, Practice

There's no shame in rehearsing what you want to say to your boss. I also recommend practicing your response if they say no, or if they decide to negotiate with you. How will you handle it? Write down your best responses and practice saying them out loud and with confidence. I would even go as far as trying to anticipate ways your boss might justify denying your request for a raise. What counterarguments will you use in return? Fake it till you make it and be as mentally prepared as possible.

Step 4: Ask on a Good Day

You probably don't want to ask for a raise on a day when projects are due or the boss is finalizing their divorce. Try to pick a time that works well for all parties involved. Ask for a closed-door meeting; don't be an Awkward Andy and ask for a raise in front of other co-workers.

Step 5: Have the Confidence of RuPaul on a Runway

Writer Sarah Hagi once tweeted, "Carry yourself with the confidence of a mediocre white man" and Lord have mercy did that resonate with women around the world. Ladies, don't you dare allow yourself to suffer from imposter syndrome any longer. You are in the position to ask for a raise because you work hard, are capable, and add tremendous value to your company. You are just as good, if not better, at what you do than your peers. Even if you don't quite believe it, present yourself in a way that makes others feel your power.

When you sit down for your meeting with the boss, be cognizant of your posture. Display professionalism in every aspect of your being, this includes speaking in a clear and confident tone.

Step 6: The Power of Positivity

Not only should you be repeating positive mantras in your head in the days leading up to your meeting, but you should also be speaking well of your company. After all, you are about to ask them for a raise. While actually asking for the raise, remain positive. Neither you nor your employer want to be left with a bad taste in the mouth.

I'm a huge nerd for self-improvement books. I've read them all. From Tony Robbins, Tim Ferriss, Brené Brown, Elizabeth Gilbert, Gretchen Rubin, Deepak Chopra, and a million others; if they wrote a self-help book there's a solid chance I read it in a year I got dumped. The common factor in most of these books is the power in positive thinking. I've really come to deeply believe the energy I put out into the world will be reciprocated. I also believe how I react to negative events and energy will shape my reality. For example, if I get turned down for a raise, it would be easy to dwell on the bad (i.e., My boss is a dick. I suck at life. I don't deserve a raise. I'm an idiot). Instead, I allow myself one day to throw a pity party, and then I reshape my perception of the negative (i.e., What can I learn from this? How can I improve my approach or skills? What other companies might find value in me where my current one doesn't?).

Sometimes my friends think I get too philosophical, which is very true if I've had any amount of alcohol. So I'll just put it this way: negative people have shitty lives and things rarely go well for them. Positive people have awesome lives because they shift bad into better, and are grateful for the good. Apply this principle to your work and professional life and you'll thrive.

Step 7: Assume the Position...No, Not That Position

Get on YouTube and watch the TED Talk by Amy Cuddy where she discusses body language. It is powerful and will make you stand a little taller. I've put a link to the video in the "Resources and Links" section.

Before you go to work on the day you ask for the raise, stand in your mirror in a power position. Make yourself as big as fucking possible. I'm talking arms in the air, head held high, feet at least shoulder width apart. Stand like this for at least two minutes. If you watched the Amy Cuddy video, you'll know there's science behind power posing, and it will increase your levels of confidence. Power pose until you can't power pose anymore! This is your day. Get that raise and celebrate!

This essay first appeared on The Scold *on December 14, 2016*

Hobbies and Volunteer Work: Be a Better Citizen and Professional

We aren't born just to pay bills and die. I know a lot of days it feels that way, but don't ever forget there's so much more to life than your daily grind. We should all try our best to give to others for a myriad of reasons. First and foremost, volunteering and giving back to the less fortunate helps make this world slightly less callous, cold, and contemptuous. Kindness is truly good for the soul. You'll feel better, and those you help will too. You really can't go wrong donating your time and skills.

Donating your money is great as well, just be sure to check out where the money is actually going. God forbid you donate to a cause only to find out it paid for some rich guys' rounds of golf. A good resource to see the inner workings of non-profit organizations, 501(c)3s, is guidestar.org. You'll be able to peruse through non-profit Form 990s, which they file each year with the IRS. I used this site a lot when I was a journalism student and was frequently flabbergasted by the wasteful spending and exorbitant salaries of several area charities. Do your research before donating money. Your dollars deserve to actually aid the causes close to your heart.

Let's talk about volunteering. For a long time, I didn't know where or how I should volunteer. I didn't know how often I should do it either. So I ended up not doing anything at all. This is not a great approach. Don't do what I did. If you're having trouble finding a way to volunteer and give back, ask yourself what strengths and skills you can provide an organization.

When you read the news, what kind of stories affect you the most? You don't have to look far outside your window to find local causes in need of volunteers. Identify one or two places where you'd like to donate your time, skill, or money. It feels amazing to give back. You don't have to save the world, but we can all get off our ass and spend an afternoon doing something for the greater good.

I think a great way to give back is mentorship. There are so many kids who need guidance and inspiration from young adults. You don't have to be a perfect person. It's enough to be someone who cares, treats everyone with respect, and tries hard in their endeavors.

I also believe adults need hobbies. Hobbies keep us young, they keep our minds sharp, and they increase our happiness. If you find yourself without a hobby, I recommend testing a variety of activities until you find something you truly enjoy. Let the process of finding a hobby be a fun adventure. My hobbies include golf, writing satire and sketch comedy, and spending an outrageous amount of time scrolling through Twitter. Not all hobbies are created equal.

Hobbies are a great escape from the monotony and stress of our everyday lives. For the majority of Americans, our workdays are stressful. Our lives are complicated and busy, and a hobby provides a much needed moment of respite. Let your hobby be an activity that relaxes you and helps recharge your battery.

Through your noble volunteer efforts and your hobbies, you will become a more empathetic, energized, efficient, and effective citizen and professional. It's weird how all those words beginning with the letter "e" so effortlessly fit into that sentence.

Why Women Should Start Businesses

Have you ever thought about starting a business? What's stopping you? Is it fear of failure? Unsure where to begin? Feel like you don't have the necessary startup capital? What's really holding you back? This is the year to take control of your life and to give away your last fucks.

According to *Forbes*, women have been starting more businesses than men for the past twenty years, and that's freaking awesome. I would like to personally encourage you to start a business. It's not for everyone, but if you're on the fence about it, I hope you'll read this and go out and start your ass- kicking entrepreneurial journey.

Here's why women should start businesses:

Flexibility

Women tend to start more home-based small businesses. Home-based businesses allow a level of flexibility not found in traditional 9-5 office jobs. While it's good to hold yourself accountable to a routine and work schedule, it's nice to be able to move working hours when necessary. I often work between the hours of 8 P.M. and 10 P.M. I'm not sure why I get a second wind during this time, but my best creative ideas and writing always happens a couple hours after dinner. Is there a scientific reason for this? I'd love to know.Hit me up if you can explain this burst of evening creative energy. I love owning a business where I have the flexibility to get shit done during the time of day when my mind is most productive. I can tell you this: I don't get much work done between 5 P.M. and 6 P.M. because *Ellen*'s on. Also, technology allows many entrepreneurs to become location independent. It's amazing to be able to pack up my laptop for a week and hit the road. I'm not always as productive as I need to be when I'm traveling, but there's something so liberating about not having to ask for vacation time.

The only downside to this level of flexibility is that it's very difficult to completely shut off from work. I rarely go a full day without doing some sort of business-related activity.

Best Way to Become Filthy Rich

I recently read an article discussing how the wealthiest people in the world are all entrepreneurs. The message of the article was that you'll never become filthy rich working for other people. It's true: you've got to forge your own path. If you work for someone else, your earning potential is capped. As an entrepreneur, earning potential is limitless. It won't be easy, but ask Bill Gates if it was worth it.

Lead By Example

You want to see real change in the world? Then let it start with you. This past year was a big wake up call for me. I realized I can't rely on other people to make things happen in my life. I recently read Sheryl Sandberg's *Lean In*. It's a great book for all women, but I was especially inspired by her willingness to lead by example. She's only one woman, but Sandberg galvanized millions with her words and actions. Women tend to minimize their capabilities so as not to appear arrogant. Your confidence is not arrogance; it's a terrific example for the other women in your life. If we all thought one person was incapable of creating real change, nothing of significance would ever be accomplished. Don't limit yourself!

Women Are Good at It

Women are intuitive. We're resilient. We're adaptable. These are perfect traits for entrepreneurship. Yes, these are gross generalizations, but if you possess these traits you're capable of starting a business. Trust me, if I can do it, anyone can. My dog is more qualified to start a business than I ever will be.

Where to begin:

Do Some Research

There are so many resources for people looking to start a business. Get info from your local chamber of commerce. Research your potential competition to see how they got started and how they're now running. Starting a business will require you to leave your comfort zone and become insatiably hungry for knowledge. You don't have to know everything about starting a business before you jump in headfirst. It's okay to learn as you go. It may be overwhelming, but you'll survive and you'll be invigorated and motivated with every new piece of information you digest.

Vision Board Your Ideas

Okay, so, I stole this one from my Lord and Savior, Oprah Winfrey. I have a vision board. It helps me organize the million thoughts in my head, and to clearly visualize my goals. It helps, and you should try it. If you have an idea, but aren't sure how you want to turn it into a tangible product or service, write that shit down. Draw pictures, jot notes, cut out magazine photos, do whatever it takes to get it out of your head and onto a vision board where you can build upon your brilliance. Vision boards are a great visual reminder of what you're actively working toward.

Talk to People

Go and find people who are already doing what you want to do and talk to them. How did they get started? How did they reach their level of success? Be curious, and ask questions. There are so many entrepreneurs willing to give advice and tips; you just have to ask politely.

Be Brave and Jump

At some point you're going to have to take a leap of faith. No matter how prepared you are, making the decision to start a business is terrifying. What's the worst that can happen? You're forced to go back to doing what you're currently doing?

There's no shame in failing, but there is shame in not trying.

If you fail, you'll be okay. There are lessons to be learned. Hold your head high, and be proud you were brave enough to follow your dreams. So, go ahead, start your business.

This essay first appeared on The Scold *on March 15, 2017*

Finding Fulfilling Work

What's your career motivation? Are you following your passion? Do you want to make as much money as possible? Are you living a life of service to others? Are you secretly in love with a coworker, à la Jim and Pam from *The Office*? Awhile back, I watched a TED Talk featuring a young man named Benjamin Todd who specializes in giving career advice. At first I was cynical. What the hell can this young goofy bastard tell me about finding a career I love that I haven't already heard a thousand times. Then the lanky young man said something that surprised me. He said, "Do what's valuable."

Benjamin continued his talk by saying if you follow what you're passionate about, you'll likely burn out or fail. Statistics prove his theory to be true. Instead, do what's valuable. Often a passion will then develop, and you'll be fulfilled professionally and personally. I was astounded. This TED Talk spurred me to bust my ass to finish this book. I'm not passionate about writing books, but if one person can apply a lesson from this guide into their life, then what I've done was well worth the effort. I will have done something of value and that feels more satisfying to me than any other job I've ever worked.

What's Valuable to Others?

You don't have to change the world with your work. If you can be of service and value to one small group or cause, that'll bring you as much personal and professional fulfillment as a millionaire writing checks to charity. Whether you're a teacher, a social worker, a non-profit employee, a fireman, a policewoman, a chef, a soldier, a nurse, or an adult entertainer, you are providing a valuable service. What's valuable to others can provide you with a selfless and satisfying career.

What Causes Do You Care About?

I care about financial literacy because I was once
financially illiterate. I want to save people from the

mistakes and traps I fell into as a young person trying to
make a life for myself. I genuinely hope that by teaching
people about personal finance, I am doing something of
value for others. What do you care about? I highly doubt
the answer is "nothing." That's an intellectually indolent
answer. Do a little soul searching and find something
outside of yourself to care about. It's surprisingly
rewarding.

Research Companies Whose Values Align With Yours

A great way to find a fulfilling career is to look for jobs
within companies that focus on the same valuable work that
interests you. Joining a team with a mission that
complements your personal values is going to keep you
motivated to do wonderful things. However you choose to
do what's valuable, there will be a company somewhere in
the world searching for a person like you.

Do I Need a Mentor?

Young professionals ask frequently if they need a mentor, or if they can survive without one. In my opinion, you don't necessarily need one, but it doesn't hurt to have a mentor. I think mentors can be more helpful in certain industries, particularly for women.

The definition of a mentor is evolving, as well. Traditionally, a mentor was a senior person with tremendous experience and knowledge who helped a junior person develop professionally. There are several variations on what a mentor in the 21st century actually entails. I'll elaborate on that later.

First, let's discuss the benefits of a mentor:

They'll Help You Build Connections

It's all about who you know right? If you and your mentor have a great relationship, they'll more than likely introduce you to others who can help advance your career. Warning: do not be that person who only uses the mentor relationship to meet higher-up people. That's gross. Don't be gross.

They'll Inspire and Motivate You

Hopefully this person will assist you in keeping your eyes on the prize. A good mentor is a source of energy from which you can keep yourself inspired and motivated.

They'll Help You Through Tough Times, Challenges, and Obstacles

Mentors are there for you to lean on and learn from. You will undoubtedly experience low points in your career. A mentor during these challenging times provides the insight necessary to help guide you through.

They'll Help You Visualize Your Future

Mentors are an example of where you'd like to be in the future, so let them help you set goals. A mentor clarifies what it is you're trying to achieve. How are you going to get anywhere if you don't have a destination in mind? A mentor assists in clearing a path for you.

They are a Dictionary, Thesaurus, and Encyclopedia

Mentors provide a wealth of information, knowledge, and expertise. Be smart enough to know you don't know anything at all. Especially early in your career, your mind should be a humble little sponge. It can be tempting to present yourself as a confident person with all the answers, but people see right through that. It's better to be quietly confident and eager to learn. A mentor helps you acquire the tools you'll need to succeed in your personal and professional life.

They Are Your Coach

Mentors will identify your strengths and weaknesses and assist you in improving upon both. Again, this is where being coachable is incredibly important. Constructive criticism can be hard to hear, but it's an imperative part in growing as a professional.

They Are Great for Brainstorming

Your mentor should be someone you bounce ideas off. If you've established a relationship with a mentor who is willing to listen to your ideas, you've hit the jackpot. Workshopping ideas with someone who has a lifetime worth of knowledge and expertise is invaluable.

They'll Protect You

Mentors can prevent you from making costly mistakes. A good mentor will warn you of pitfalls and traps. Don't be someone who constantly chooses to learn lessons the hard way.

So how do you find a mentor you ask? It's not like asking someone out on a date. You do not want to approach someone and simply ask them to be your mentor without first establishing a relationship. You should also let them know this isn't a one-way street. Find out how you can provide value to them in return.

There are people out there who want to help you and who want to see you succeed. You just can't be an obnoxious douche about it. A mentor-mentee relationship should be grown organically. Start by identifying someone you admire and respect. Let them know how you feel about them without kissing their ass too much. Nourish and cultivate the relationship by offering to take them to lunch, ask them if you can assist with one of their projects, or let them know you're interested in learning from them. Again, be genuine about it and not a weirdo brown nose.

I don't believe the mentor-mentee relationship has to be formal, either. A mentor doesn't have to be someone who works in your industry. A mentor can be anyone you truly respect. It can be a co-worker whose work ethic and process you observe. A mentor can be a radio or podcast personality, an author, a speaker, a leader, etc. A mentor can be someone you know personally, or someone you admire from afar, which is why I tell people Oprah is my mentor. I also have mentors whom I've actually met in real life. It's all about finding people you can learn from and who will inspire you to be the best version of yourself.

Finally, if you're going to have a mentor, you need to be willing to listen and take advice. Why would someone waste their time on you if you're going to be combative, argumentative, and not receptive to their counsel? You have to be coachable. It's okay if you don't always agree with your mentor, but be respectful and grateful for the time they'vespent on you.

Again, I don't think success is impossible without a mentor. More important than having someone who can guide you through life, is having the right attitude. A willingness to learn, listen, and grow will naturally attract people who will want to push your career to the next level. Remember to be grateful to those who mentor you and always say "thank you."

This Job Is Just a Stepping-Stone

Every job is a stepping-stone. Whether we make up, down, or lateral career moves, each new role will provide you with a life lesson. Every job offers the opportunity to build new skills and make you a more valuable employee. More times than not, finding the value and lesson in a job will depend on your attitude and willingness to learn.

Try Not to Burn Bridges

At some point in your life, I guarantee you will have a job that will suck ass. You'll wake up every morning dreading the next eight hours and count the moments until you can taste that freedom of happy hour. You may also hate your coworkers and wish the plague upon your boss. As badly as you want to burn your cubicle to the ground, try your best not to burn bridges with coworkers and managers. When you're able to move on from this employment hell, there are a few reasons you don't want to flip your boss the bird and steal all the company pens on your way out. First, we live in a small world and people talk. You don't want any negative rumors to reach your new place of employment before you even get there. Secondly, you don't want to be blacklisted in an industry. People are vindictive and seek revenge in the form of telling other companies not to hire you. Finally, kill everyone with kindness. Try your best not to leave a job on a negative note. It's bad for you mentally, spiritually, and is a complete energy drain. Although you may not see eye to eye with your boss or coworkers, you may one day need them as a reference or you might run into them on Tinder.

Be Cognizant of What Aspects of the Job Make You Happy and What Do Not

What is it about your current job that you don't like? Is it the long hours? Are you not being challenged? Do you want to strangle Bethany in accounting? Is Barry sending sexual emails again? Write down the pros and cons of your current role. Ask yourself what you like, what can be improved, and what you absolutely cannot stand. Instead of just settling for, "I fucking hate this job," you're better served if you can isolate exactly what you don't like and see if it is within your control to change or improve.

As you grow in your career, have a list of things you really love within a role and company and things you won't deal with again. This list will help you formulate questions to ask during future interviews to see if a company is a good fit for you or not.

Develop Your Skills

Even if you're a 25 year old CEO wunderkind, you aren't perfect and there are abilities you need to develop and new knowledge to acquire. What can you work on at your current stepping-stone job? The answer might not pop out at you right away, but I guarantee you that you can find something in which you can develop expertise. Take the time at your current job to improve yourself and you'll be glad you did once you're in a role you desire.

Try to Enjoy Your Time There

A positive attitude goes a long way. Trust me, I know how awful it is to wake up each morning and get ready to head to an office you don't want to sit in. There were days I would've literally rather punched myself in the face for a week straight than answer phone calls and emails while listening to a coworker brag about her amazing boyfriend who obviously was cheating on her. There were times I let my negative attitude completely ruin each and every day, and it even bled into my weekends. By Sunday night, I could feel the anxiety and stress building in my chest and I longed for the next Friday at 5 P.M. That's no way to live, my friends. Do what you can to put yourself into a positive mindset. Meditate for a few minutes in the morning or at night before you go to bed. Take a yoga class on the weekends. Do breathing exercises when you feel yourself getting worked up at your desk. There are a million great books to help you de-stress and think positive thoughts, even when it feels impossible. Make the best of your circumstances. I know it's easier said than done.

Don't Downplay or Discount the Importance of Your Current Role

You may look back 30 years from now and wish you had done things differently. The role you're in right now seems insignificant, but sometimes you don't appreciate your contributions and added value until much later. You still need to take your job seriously. I don't care how menial you think your job is in the hierarchy of the company; it's a poor reflection on you and your character if you aren't trying. If you don't want to try for your company, your boss, or your coworkers, then do it for yourself. Push yourself to be the best version of you even when no one is looking or outwardly expressing their appreciation for your time and effort. Your work ethic, contributions, and value won't always be recognized. That's just a fact of life. But don't let yourself down. Take your job seriously and know that even the low man on the totem pole has a mission to accomplish.

You're Never Stuck

This is a piece of advice my mom gives my sister and I during the most challenging periods of our lives. Whether we were in an unhealthy relationship, a job we hated, an apartment with bad roommates, our mom provided us a sense of hope with the simple phrase: you are never stuck.

If you don't like your situation, be brave enough to change it. Yes, you should honor commitments and don't get into a habit of quitting everything as soon as it becomes difficult or unpleasant. But also don't torture yourself. Life is fleeting. Why should we waste our precious moments on this earth being miserable and in situations that drown us in negativity? A lot of old school people tell me this is the Millennial snowflake mentality. I call bullshit. Look at the big picture of your life. What are you going to regret more? Going after what you really want and perhaps failing? Or staying stuck in a situation, personally or professionally, that is soul-crushing? I think it's cowardly to allow yourself to remain stuck anywhere. There's a lot more that's within our control than we acknowledge. When your heart is telling you that you need to make a change, listen to it.

The Elusive Work-Life Balance

There are so many damn opinions on work-life balance. For real though, what the hell is work-life balance? Do you know what it means? I've been trying to define it for years. Here's what I've come up with: work-life balance means enjoying a fulfilling career that also affords ample time for the people and hobbies I value most.

I once heard the advice, "You can have it all, it just depends on what your definition of 'all' is." How fucking true is that? I'm so glad I heard that phrase in my twenties because it has profoundly shaped how I view the "big picture" of my life and career.

Take a moment to think about how you would define "having it all." Your definition is unique to you. My personal philosophy on the work-life balance is based on goals. Goals give us a focus and a purpose, they allow us to shape our lives in such a way that we're accomplishing what we want both professionally and personally. My goal was to publish this book and then go on a nice vacation. One professional goal followed by one personal goal. To me, that's achieving some level of balance.

Your work-life balance is defined by what you prioritize. As your life gets more complicated and busy, your ability to prioritize will determine if you have any semblance of a work- life balance. When you feel good about the amount of working and living you're doing, you'll have a sense of fulfillment and contentment. Your work-life balance may shift as your life evolves, but it's important to remember to stay true to yourself and your personal values.

If you're struggling with understanding work-life balance within your own existence, here are some tips that may clarify and encourage you to live your best life:

Prioritize and Make Choices

Indecision is a huge waste of time. If you truly want work-life balance, you need to know what aspects of your personal and professional life need prioritization. I know I sound like I'm beating a dead horse when I tell you to write these things down, but write down what's most important to you. Are Sunday afternoon dinners with your family important? If so, write it down. Is leaving the office most nights by 6 P.M. so you can make it to your kid's game important? Write it down. Is exercising four times a week or taking a yoga class a priority for you? Then write it down, you beautiful mess, you.

You're going to have to make choices. Do you work late and miss your friend's birthday dinner? I don't know, that depends on your priorities. Either way, you have to make a choice and there will be sacrifices. It's a crappy part of life, but we all only have 24 hours a day and seven days a week.

Exercise and Meditate

Exercising sucks so hard. I'm not sure I'll ever be able to wake up at 5 A.M. and hit the gym. I'm not one of those people. I prefer a nice lunchtime class or an evening yoga. You don't have to torture yourself to get in shape and be a relatively healthy person. Find a form of exercise you can enjoy, or at least tolerate, and do that a few times per week.

Meditation works wonders as well. If transcendental meditation isn't your cup of tea, just find ten minutes a day to sit quietly and focus on your breathing. The simple act of consciously breathing and decompressing can lower your stress levels and anxiety. There are a million resources in books and on the Internet that will tell you how to meditate if you've never done it before.

Put Your Phone Away for One Fucking Minute

You have to unplug in order to reach the ultimate levels of

work-life balance. I frequently find myself sitting at family picnics checking my work email on my phone. This is nonsense. When I do this, I'm not fully engaged in my work, and I'm also not present among my family. Put down your phone and disconnect from technology when you are in the presence of your loved ones. Memories are made in person, not through your iPhone.

Identify and Eliminate Your Biggest "Time Wasters"

I think we can all agree our excessive and mindless scrolling through social media is our number one time waster. The average American now spends five hours per day on their mobile device. That is probably the most insane statistic I've ever read. Do you know how much we could accomplish in five hours? What if we cut our social media and cell phone usage down by an hour? Our productivity would skyrocket. It's virtually impossible to totally disconnect in this day and age, but I think if we took small steps to decrease our social media usage, our work-life balance would dramatically improve. Oh, and it'll probably restore our attention spans which are now comparable to squirrels.

Surround Yourself with People Who Support You

Your family and friends should understand the pressures and stresses in your life. You need to communicate to them what your schedule looks like and how you're doing your best to balance your professional expectations with your personal ones. Surround yourself with people who appreciate you and want the best for you. Be with people who bring positivity into your life and lessen the sting of the personal and professional sacrifices you make every day. A good support system won't abandon you when you need them most and they'll help you reach the level of work-life balance you so desire.

I don't care what path you choose, you're going to make sacrifices. Whether you're a stay-at-home parent or working full-time, life is full of tiny daily sacrifices. Accept that you can't be everything to everyone and you definitely won't be everywhere at all times. This is a fact of life, and you shouldn't feel bad about it. You can't control how many hours are in a day. You can't control traffic. You can't control the weather.

You can, however, control yourself and how you react to adversity. You can control what you prioritize and how you choose to spend your time. Your level of productivity is mostly up to you. If you choose to spend an hour scrolling Facebook, and then are angry when it's 5 P.M. on Friday and you're still working to meet a deadline, that's all on you, my friend. Learn to manage yourself, your emotions, and your time wisely. When you manage yourself well, you'll manage your work-life balance even better. Now let's go get a drink.

Job Hopping: The Good, The Bad, and The Struggle of Being a 20-Something

When my parents were young, company loyalty was vital. A person in their 20s or 30s who didn't stay at a job for more than a few years was painted as a liability and a problem to avoid when hiring. In recent years, that thinking has shifted quite drastically. In the age of startups and ever-changing work landscapes, someone who has bounced around is now perceived as a person looking for growth, a challenge, and healthy risks.

If you're thinking about switching jobs, or even careers, there are many pros and cons to consider. Let's start with the pros:

A New and Exciting Endeavor

If you're bored with your current position, the idea of moving to another job is exciting. This new company could provide you with endless professional fulfillment. New challenges, such as changing jobs, bring us out of our comfort zone. Being out of our comfort zone forces us to develop new skills and abilities more rapidly than we would otherwise. Changing a job or career is an excellent opportunity for self-development.

An Opportunity for Growth

Recent studies show switching jobs can help increase your salary at a faster rate than staying with one company, particularly early in your career. If you're taking a job with a new company, it could be a chance for you to move up the ranks a little more quickly.

You're a Unique Snowflake

You'll have a wide variety of experience and knowledge if

you work for different companies. Every company is different, so you'll become great at quickly adapting to a new environment. People who embrace change instead of fearing it are much more confident in their personal and professional lives.

There are potential downsides as well. Let's have a look at the cons:

People and Employers Will Still Question Your Motives and Staying Power

Not everyone is like you. There are people in this world who are quitters and simply can't hold a job. Employers are still wary of this when they see short job durations on resumes. If you have moved around quite a bit, be ready to explain why. The interviewer won't know about the skills you've learned and the value you'll add to their team unless you make it clear.

You May Lose Stock Options/Employer Contributions

Hopefully if you're taking a new job, you'll see an increase in salary and benefits. If you leave your current position there's a possibility you will lose stock options and employer contributions to your retirement plan. Remember, you only get to keep the vested balance. Check and make sure you know what's yours to keep before jumping ship.

Is This Job Actually Better?

If you're looking to leave your old job because you're unhappy, you may jump at the chance to work elsewhere. But is this new company really better? How much do you know about them? Are you taking a pay cut? Is this new job going to provide the same, better, or worse work-life balance? Also, by job-hopping, you might not be giving yourself the opportunity to really get to know your current company and its inner workings. Are there opportunities you could be missing with your current employer? These are all questions you need to ask yourself before making a big move.

This essay first appeared on The Funny Financial Planner *blog on August 30, 2016*

Don't Be a Jerk

"Nice guys finish last." How many times have you heard that asinine saying in your lifetime? The answer is, "too many." Let's debunk this myth. You do not need to be an asshole to succeed professionally. If you don't believe me read Adam Grant's *Give and Take: Why Helping Others Drives Our Success.* He offers evidence to show people who are generous with their time, contacts, and knowledge are the most dominant in their fields. This is a departure from the misconception that the overconfident asshole always comes out on top.

Of course, there will be jerks who ascend to the top of the corporate ladder in every industry, but let them be the exception and not the rule. Our world is already poisoned with negative personalities; let's not make it worse.

Here's how I see it: your career is important, but it isn't everything. There's more to life than what you do for a living. Your career won't define you, but how you treat people will. So don't be an asshole.

When I think about those cutthroat types who believe the only way to reach the C-suite is to step on others, I feel bad for them. If you think that you have to cut down people to get ahead in this world, you're really missing out on the best of what life has to offer.

I encourage you to be competitive. There's nothing wrong with pushing yourself and creating an environment where you and your colleagues are making one another better. But, compete with fairness and integrity. Your integrity is invaluable. If you cheat, and even if you get away with it, someday it'll come back to bite you in the ass.

So, instead of lowering yourself and utilizing butthole tactics to get ahead in the workforce, what can you do instead? "Great question, thank you for asking," I utter to myself in a very meta and lonely moment during the construction of this book.

First, I encourage you to be true to your values and never compromise what you believe in, even if that means occasionally being stern with people. Stand up for yourself and your beliefs in a way that is both respectful and assured. As tempting as it is, don't allow yourself to throw cheap shots, low blows, or be passive-aggressive. I'm actively working on my passive-aggression, because I know it's a problem, but I also know you deserved a lot of those eye rolls.

Second, I encourage you to spread positivity, because that'll take you further than a negative attitude ever will. When I was a sophomore in college I read a book called *The Secret* and most of it was *Looney-Tunes*-level weird, but the parts that discussed the laws of attraction really impacted how I conducted myself in the world. I know the energy you put out into the world will be reciprocated, whether you choose positivity or negativity. You have a choice to respond to every situation and event in your life in love or fear. You won't always choose correctly, but do your best to put out more goodness than not.

Finally, if you feel like you have to be an asshole to get ahead, ask yourself what you are truly gaining. Do your peers and those who work for you respect you more? Are you trying to get more people to listen or do their jobs better? I guarantee you, the asshole approach is not the most effective or efficient. Instead of cultivating an environment of productivity and cooperation, you'll end up with an office full of resentment and catty attitudes.

You want respect? Good morale? To be the CEO? Try being kind, helpful, competent, competitive, positive, generous, and reliable. Choose to be a lifter of people instead of cutting everyone down. Never confuse fear with respect. Let's say it one more time for the people in the back: "Don't be an asshole!"

Part III: Essays on Relationships

I've spent a considerable amount of time deciding what I want to cover in these relationship essays. I'm not a love guru, but I am a human woman who has experienced both the highs and lows of dating. I know what it's like to have your heart broken and to be the heartbreaker. I know how uncomfortable it is to be on a first date and the questions that arise when you decide to take a relationship to the next level. You might not agree with all my conclusions and that's fine. I'd still like to discuss with you what I've learned in the years since I got my first kiss on a couch at my best friend's house. I was 26. I'm kidding, I was 13 with uneven bangs, cystic acne, and crooked teeth. I was a real stunner in those days.

I think it's important to spend a little time discussing dating in a digital world. The infiltration of technology in our search for a mate is both fascinating and complex. The way we interact with one another is constantly evolving. Will we even go on dates in 20 years? Then of course there's age-old topics including marriage, starting a family, and everyone's favorite taboo subject: sex.

We'll talk about types of relationships, how to break up with people, and how to keep the spice alive, among several other things. I hope you'll find this section of the book to be the most hilarious, uncomfortable, and absolutely relatable. I also know my dad is going to read this at some point so let me just say this: Dad, for you the book ends at this sentence. For the rest of you, let's dive deep into this confusing as hell world of relationships and have a little fun.

Dating in a Digital Century

Can you imagine if your grandma and grandpa met on
Tinder? I'm sure some of your grandparents got down on the
first date, but back then they didn't have a thirsty as fuck
online bio. They were thirsty in private, big difference.
Someday, our generation will explain that we met grandma
or grandpa on a dating app built for casual sex. I think our
society will be so evolved by that point it won't make a
difference to our grandkids. One time my grandpa, rest his
soul, said something about sex with my grandma at our
Christmas dinner and I very nearly threw myself out the
window in disgust. I'm looking forward to making the same
joke 50 years from now, but hopefully my grandkids won't
react as poorly as I did.

Dating in this century is rapidly evolving and I think we
should continue to embrace the technology that's bringing
our private parts together. With that being said, I also think
we need to remember the following: who someone says they
are in an online bio is not at all who they really are in
person. Nothing will ever replace face-to-face interaction.

I read somewhere that Millennials and the following
generations are going out less and less. We are so
"connected" to our technological world that we feel no need
to be connected to our physical world. This is sad. I've
gotten to know a lot of people through Twitter and
Facebook, but hanging out with friends in real life are the
memories I cherish most. Our memories now will be us
looking at screens. That's just not as fun or, frankly,
memorable.

Use technology to help filter out people you want to get to
know better from those you don't. Beyond that, don't let
apps and screen time take away from interactions in real
life.

I wouldn't rely exclusively on technology to find a partner either. There's a biological factor in finding a compatible person to date. You're not going to get a whiff of someone's pheromones via Tinder or Match.

Studies Show People Who Use Online Dating Go on More Dates

If you want to increase your date frequency, getting a profile up online is probably your best bet. This does raise the question: are you more about quality or quantity? There's no wrong answer, it's just about discovering your motives. Do you think your chances of finding a spouse will increase if you go on a ton of dates? Or, are you just interested in meeting a lot of people and perhaps also having sex with a lot of people? I believe online dating can accomplish any of the above. Which segues to the next point:

Be Clear About What You're Looking for (Hookups vs. Relationships)

You should not only be honest with yourself, but you should be upfront with the people you're going on dates with. Are you looking for a casual hookup or an actual relationship? Again, there's no wrong answer here; it's more about being fair to the other person. They have the right to know your intentions, just like you have the right to know theirs.

Don't Get Overwhelmed by Your Options (Either Too Many or Not Enough)

I don't care what dating site you're on, there are likely thousands of candidates waiting for your confirmation or rejection. This is overwhelming. The sheer number of potential hookups/boyfriends/girlfriends/spouses is enough to make you question if there's really such a thing as "the one." Or, maybe the magnitude of people available on these sites and your continual singleness has left you wondering, "What the hell is wrong with me? Why can't I find anyone in this sea of horniness?" Don't let the hugeness of this digital dating sphere get you down. Your self-worth is not measured in swipes right.

The Actual Relationship Shouldn't be Through Your Phone

Your relationships should develop organically and in person and it feels super fucking weird to have to write that, but hey, it's the 21st century. When you do match with someone, please put your Goddamn phone down while in each other's physical presence. We humans still need to get to know one another through actual face-to-face communication. Don't rely on texting or another form of messaging to learn about somebody. How can you tell if you are truly into a person until you're sitting on the couch and one of you lets it rip? You can't get that make or break moment through text messaging.

If It's Not Working Out, Break up and Move on

You guys. Our time on this earth is precious and fleeting. If the person you're dating isn't panning out, please cut ties as gracefully as possible and move the hell on. Don't waste your time on a dead-end relationship. It's not fair to you or the other person.

Be Really Freaking Careful

We've all watched *Catfish*. Nev Schulman ruined online romance for all of us. Maybe Nev and his perfect smile were trying to raise awareness of a common digital romance scam, but he just scared the bejesus out of all of my friends and me.

This is a weird new world we're living in. Only 20 years ago, the idea of swiping left or right would've sent our permed-hair ancestors into a frenzy. Don't people meet organically after three beers in a bar anymore? Maybe I'm too negative about this dating in a digital age. Maybe I'm turning into a crusty old bag. Yeah, that's probably it. I'm a a crusty old bag.

Types of Relationships Available to You

Let's take a moment to discuss the types of consensual relationships you can enter into as an adult human being. It's important to know what kind of relationship for which you are best suited. I don't care what kind of relationship you're in, they all require a certain level of work and open communication.

Monogamy

A monogamous relationship is the most basic and traditional of relationship categories available to you. Many believe monogamy is not inherently natural, thus it requires a level of commitment and willpower. Monogamy has its pros and cons. I've only been in monogamous relationships. Well, at least they were monogamous on my part. I'm not bitter, I just wish a plague would descend upon those who have betrayed me. I'm fine you guys. Pros of monogamy include building a bond with one special person. Monogamous relationships are rewarding and fulfilling if they are with a compatible partner. Obviously, if you're monogamous, you're only sleeping with that one person. Some might say this is both a pro and a con.

Polygamy

Polygamous relationships tend to be more closely linked to certain religious affiliations and generally refer to a man taking multiple wives. When I think about polygamy, I immediately think of that weird show *Sister Wives*. I've never actually met anyone in a polygamous marriage, but it's apparent that polygamy is more work than I care to take on. Marriage is hard enough as it is, but having to evenly split your time among several wives and the wives needing to all get along is exhausting. But then again, I think I could handle being sister wives with my best friends. Like how cool would it be to drink wine and talk shit about your spouse with your best friend every night? If this is how polygamy works, I might be interested. I just don't want to live in a rural part of Utah. Also, I really don't think this is how polygamy works.

Polyamorous

Polyamory means "many loves." Someone who is polyamorous can be in multiple relationships at one time. I actually know a few polyamorous people and it works for them. The important thing is to be open and honest with your partners, and from what I've heard, polyamorous people are pretty great at communicating within their relationships.

Single and Loving It

I also know several awesome women who are single and fucking love it. I also know several men who are doing the same. But for whatever reason, society is always way cooler about single men than they are single women. The women I know who are killing it, own their singleness. They don't place their value in whether or not they're in a relationship. They're self-assured, successful, and will not settle for less than they deserve. They're confident that whether they meet someone or if they remain single, they'll continue living their best life.

Single and Hating It

If you're single and hating it there could be several reasons why. First, I know it's human nature to want to share your life with someone. I get it. But if finding love isn't happening as quickly as you'd hoped, please know you are not a failure and your life does not suck and you aren't going to die an old smelly cat hoarder. Or, maybe you will. There's nothing wrong with cat ladies.

My advice to the people who are single and hating it is to stop looking. Stop it. Focus on yourself. Focus on your own personal joy. Focus on your career. Focus on your mind and your body and your spiritual well being. One of two things will happen. You'll either become one of the people who are single and loving it, or you might just find yourself attracting a mate because you're happy and healthy. Either way, you're winning.

Open Relationships

An open relationship is when partners agree that they each can hook up with other people. If you don't have consent from everyone within the relationship, then it's just cheating. Open relationships have to be agreed upon before you can partake in one. Again, honest and open communication is key.

Swingers

I've never met swingers in real life, but I know they exist. Swinging is when couples have sex with other couples. If everyone involved is cool with it, then go ahead and do your thing. I do know a couple who claim they were once approached to swing with another couple; out of respect for their privacy I'll refrain from using their real names, but let's just call them "my mom and dad." "My mom and dad" are old school and pretty naive, so they didn't realize they were being approached to swing until it became painfully obvious. This was on St. Patrick's Day and they just thought this couple was overly friendly. At the end of the night, when it was obvious this couple wanted to take them home, "my mom and dad" panicked and ran out of the place. At first, I was like "oh wow, this is a weird story to tell you daughter." Now I just think it's hilarious. Swingers are more common than you think, but they're also stealthy as fuck.

The Unhealthy Ex

The unhealthy ex is the result of a failed relationship that doesn't have closure. So, whenever one person gets drunk, they'll send a regrettable text to the other. This was a common trend for me and my friends throughout our twenties. I would not recommend this type of relationship; it rarely ends well. The unhealthy ex relationship is always exacerbated by alcohol and social media stalking after midnight. You know you're guilty of this. Don't lie to me.

Friends with Benefits

The friends with benefits situation seems somewhat unrealistic to me. I know there are thousands of people who disagree. There has to be some sort of underlying attraction to the other person. You like them enough to hook up with them, right? So are you really friends or is this an unexplored or unrequited love? Eventually, one of you will move on. You likely won't move on at the same time, which means somebody will get hurt. If you are able to turn those emotions off and can actually handle a no-strings attached deal, then good for you. That's no easy task. Either way, if you choose to just be friends with benefits, there still needs to be a lot of communication about expectations.

Friends without Benefits

This is a platonic relationship. Some of the most rewarding relationships in my life are with my friends. I love them dearly. Then of course there are friends who wish they had benefits, but don't. To these people I say, go ahead and express your true feelings or move along.

I'm sure there are many other relationship options, and I've only touched upon a few. Whatever type of relationship you're in, just make sure you're happy and it's always 100% consensual. You do you and always practice safe sex.

Sex: You Can Always Do It Better

I spent a long time contemplating whether or not to include
an essay on sex. One day it dawned on me: how can I write a
book about relationships and getting your shit together and
not mention something as ubiquitous as sex?

Sex is a skillful art. It's like a sport, and none of us are even
close to being the LeBron James or Serena Williams of
intercourse. You probably think you're a decent player,
maybe even a professional, but you can always be better.
Sure, you may bring your partner to completion each time,
but stay humble and don't let your sexual prowess fade over
time. Every now and again it doesn't hurt to ask what you
can do to improve your game. Learn to respond to your
partner's body. Your lover (I despise that term) deserves
your best effort each and every time. I also believe whatever
energy you're putting out into the world, you're going to get
back in spades. By this I mean, the harder you try for your
partner, the more your partner is going to want to please you
in return. It's a win-win.

A few tips I think we can all agree on:

Use tongue in moderation. Too much tongue and you might
as well let your golden retriever do the job. It's fucking
disgusting. I don't want to feel slobbery spittle running
down any part of my body. There's nothing worse than
having your neck and ears kissed gently, only to have your
partner then stick their tongue down your ear canal. This is
not hot; this is a wet willie and it should never be seen
outside of a middle school classroom. Please, learn how to
properly use your tongue. Less is more, and more is a dog
kiss.

Which segues into my second point: never underestimate the
power of a good kiss. In our society, the emphasis is always
on the sex itself, but let's not discount the impact of good

foreplay. We've all experienced at least a few terrible kissers. Unless you're one of those people who doesn't kiss until you get married. Did you all see that TV show a few years back? Where they didn't get their first kiss until their wedding day?

Absolute disaster. I'm not saying I'm an expert on kissing, but I know a quality smooch when I get one and I'm pretty confident in my own ability. Let me be real with you: I've got an okay-looking face but lips made for kissing. Passionate kisses are great, overly aggressive kisses are not. Know the difference. There are levels to kissing depending on what kind of mood you and your partner are in. There are soft and sweet kisses, there are passionate kisses, and there are tear off my clothes ASAP kisses. Your kissing will set the tone for what kind of sex you're going to have, so choose wisely.

Get on the same passion page. If one partner is in the mood for sensual and soft stimulation while the other is feeling a more *Fifty Shades of Grey* vibe, then the experience isn't going to be the best for either party involved. Sometimes you may need to be blindfolded and gagged; I don't know your life. Or, maybe you just need a Richard Gere on a piano *Pretty Woman*-style romping. You do you, friend. No judgments here. Just try to get on the same level as your sex buddy.

Confidence is sexy. Again, this applies to all humans in any type of relationship. Confidence in the sack is a turn-on. It's normal for all of us to go through times when we don't feel super hot in the bedroom. Maybe it's because of our bodies, maybe we feel disconnected from our partner, maybe you're just in a rut. It's normal, it happens, don't let yourself get stuck there. Sex is supposed to be fun.

Don't be afraid to try new things, but only if you're comfortable and it's mutually agreed upon. What I'm saying is, if you're stuck in a sex rut, get out of it by trying something new. If you try any tips out of *Cosmopolitan*, you'll end up laughing so hard you'll nearly pee yourself. No one takes your sex tips seriously *Cosmo*, no one. Maybe just a change of location will be enough to reignite your fire. You might find doing something new and surprising is exactly what you need to regain your own confidence and/or reconnect with your love. If you do relocate your lovemaking, remember not all places are created equal. Locations you should never have sex include the beach and hot tubs. The former is only good if you're trying to exfoliate your labia and the latter is like soaking in a watery infection.

Communication is the key to consistent orgasms. If you like or dislike certain moves or actions by your partner, let them know. They want to please you. You want to please them. Talk about what feels good. What's the point in having sex if you aren't both getting the most out of it? For real, don't be embarrassed to chat a little. We're all adults here and orgasms are good for your health.

Most importantly, sex should make you feel good physically, spiritually, and emotionally. Find someone to sleep with who satisfies all three. So those are my sex tips. That's all I've got. I tried to keep it as simple and straightforward as possible. I'm not going to go out and tell you to buy some weird sex toy or one of those pieces of furniture specifically built for fucking. These tips apply to everyone, too. I wish I had more to offer, but sex is a lot like sports in my mind. We should keep practicing to get better. Don't stop improving your game until a sexual partner tells you you're the Michael Jordan of intercourse. Only then have you reached life's ultimate goal.

The Proverbial Asshole and Why We Keep Dating Them

There's an epidemic plaguing us. I don't know the medical term for it, but it's characterized by our insatiable need to date horrible people. There's something about the thrill of the chase and trying to mold fuckboys and fuckgirls in our image that makes dating assholes so fun.

If you are someone who time and again is attracted to people who treat you like dirt, let's talk about the reasons why. Because, once you're able to recognize the signs and symptoms of dating an asshole, you can then correct the issue and find someone worthy of your time. Or perhaps, you're the asshole and you can start working on yourself.

First you need to know the telltales signs of an asshole:

Assholes Play Hard to Get

I'm not talking about people who don't show interest in dating you. An asshole will give you attention, flirt with you, go out on dates with you, and then tell you they aren't interested in "getting serious." They love to be chased because it's filling a void and they're insecure. They love the sense of power they feel when they sleep with you and then don't return your texts. People who play like they're unavailable are beneath you.

Assholes are Emotionally Unavailable

Someone who is emotionally available wants to get close to you. They want to share their thoughts and intentions. Emotionally available people are there for you and lend an ear when you're troubled. Assholes are the opposite of this. They won't allow themselves to feel vulnerable or express their true feelings. They shut down honest communication. They are unwilling to listen or validate how you're feeling, as well.

Assholes are Manipulative

Man, are there a lot of manipulative people out there. Manipulators are characterized by their calculated attempts to control your thoughts and actions in order to exert control. Manipulators always have an ulterior agenda and motive. They are sneaky fucks who shouldn't be trusted.

Assholes Hurt Your Feelings

This is the most obvious of the asshole red flags. Anyone who consistently hurts you emotionally deserves a metaphorical cunt punch and to never be spoken to again. Surround yourself with people who lift you up and make you feel great.

Here are a few reasons people are attracted to assholes:

They're Physically Attractive

Every single time. The most attractive human in any public space is also likely the worst. If they happen to be a sweetheart, well, I call that an anomaly. I'm a hard six in Boston, a four in New York, and a 2.5 in L.A., still I've managed to date some pretty solid-looking people. Unfortunately, as they got hotter, the less likely they were to offer to pay for dinner or actually even show up for dinner. Still, looks and a great body make us humans do stupid things. Self-aware good-looking people know they have this power.

They Know How to Pull You in

"Oh, you enjoy reading feminist literature and you drink La Croix? Me too." See what I did there? I just got you to sleep with me because I told you what you wanted to hear. Actually, I prefer Polar Seltzer and narcissistic celebrity memoirs, so I lied to you because I knew I could pull you in.

This is what assholes do. Assholes will pretend to like what you like and sweet-talk you until your panties magically remove themselves from your body. Beware of the super-charmer. They're the cousin of the manipulator.

Assholes are Confident

Humans are attracted to confidence. Confidence mixed with humility is what we should be looking for in a partner, yet we settle for false confidence that's actually narcissism or arrogance. Self-confidence is never a license to act like a complete dickwad. Don't give these people a free pass. Call them out on their shitty behavior, and definitely don't sleep with them.

Nice People are Boring

Can we just admit that assholes are more fun? The catch is that the novelty wears thin and eventually wears out completely. Nice people may not provide the same adrenaline rush, but they're more dependable and tolerable to be around for long periods of time. Assholes are like roller coasters, they're fun for about two minutes but soon you'll find yourself hanging upside down, screaming for mercy, and becoming more nauseous by the second.

The world is divided into three groups: nice people, occasional assholes, and total assholes. We now know we need to avoid total assholes. We are done with them! We're never looking back! Occasional assholes are sneaky. They're nice 50% of the time. Then something sets them off and they turn into total assholes for a period. Occasional assholes are passive- aggressive and the type that'll talk behind your back. Beware of them. Some occasional assholes can be rehabilitated by telling them, "Hey, you're really being an asshole right now. Cool the fuck out." Nice people aren't as rare as you might think. They're out there; you've just got to be patient and willing to look for them. Nice people deserve to be with someone kindhearted too. If you think you might be an occasional asshole, or God forbid, a total asshole, it's not too late for you to change your ways.

Always remember what the insightful and brilliant Maya Angelou said: "When someone shows you who they are, believe them the first time." And then remember what I always say, "Stop fucking assholes." Both poignant and insightful quotes.

Breaking up Is Hard to Do

Heartbreak is universal. Ending a relationship, whether of your own accord or involuntarily, is painful, emotional, and a real kick to the gut. Unfortunately, the odds of experiencing a breakup at least once in your life are extremely high. I only know one couple that's stayed together since high school. They are the unicorn of relationships: together at 15 and they'll probably die holding hands when they're 93. This *Notebook*- style fairytale just isn't in the cards for the majority of us. In fact, you're more likely to have multiple failed relationships over the course of your life, particularly in your 20s and 30s. A crucial part of getting your shit together in young adulthood is knowing when to break up. This doesn't just apply to relationships either. Friendships, jobs, and circumstances may all occasionally need to be kicked to the curb. As you mature, you'll find breaking up isn't easy, but if your instincts are telling you something's not right, a breakup is best for your long-term health.

If you're unhappy in any type of relationship, examine the reasons why you've stayed thus far. Do you fear the impending pain and fallout from the breakup? Is it because you don't want to hurt the other person? Are you staying for financial reasons? Are you afraid of disappointing others? These are all valid concerns, but there's one question that takes priority: what about your personal happiness? If you choose to stay in a relationship, friendship, or job that is bringing you no joy, are you giving the best of yourself? If you're unhappy, it's not just unfair to you, it's unfair to the others involved.

Don't Stay Because You Feel Like You Can't Do Any Better

Man, oh, man, do we see this a lot. I understand the concept of "settling." Life is so freaking hard. When you finally find a steady job, boyfriend/girlfriend, or just someone who will hang out with you on the weekends, it's easy to think you can't do any better. This stems from a lack of self-esteem. If we truly valued ourselves and our time we wouldn't allow ourselves to settle. You deserve what's good in this world and don't ever forget it.

Don't Stay Because of Societal Pressure

Holy shit, how is societal pressure to get married, have kids, and be loyal to one company still a thing? Your life will be full of so many more possibilities once you let go of the societal constructs limiting your potential and happiness. When you start to feel that pressure from family or friends, take a breath and remember that it's their issue, not yours. Worry about yourself and don't you dare let others make you feel bad about it.

Don't Stay Because You Don't Want to Be Alone

There's a difference between being alone and being lonely. Loneliness is defined as sadness because one has no friends or company. I don't think that's you. Being alone has its perks. Don't be scared of being alone. Have the confidence in yourself to know that you'll be okay. I truly savor my time alone. It gives me the rare opportunity to pick my nose and drink wine without fear of judgment.

Let It Be a Lesson

With each breakup, you should at least be jotting mental notes of what you're looking for in a partner, what you can do better in the next relationship, and adding to your list of deal breakers. If you recently broke up with a friend or a company, you can essentially do this same thing. Now, I'm not saying you should expect perfection from the next person you date, but you should have a better idea of who you are and your non-negotiable values.

Of course, if you are in an abusive situation, whether it's verbal, emotional, or physical, please seek help. If you feel you are trapped, there are resources out there for you. You are not alone. The National Domestic Abuse hotline is available 24-7 and can be reached at 1-800-799-7233.

Keeping the Spice Alive: Making Long-Term Relationships Work

Hold onto your pants, I'm going to talk about sex again. The longer you're in a relationship with someone, the more likely you are to fall into what I call the monotony of monogamy. Monogamy is a choice and not necessarily something humans are biologically inclined to prefer. Thus, keeping the spice alive in your long-term relationship is a concerted effort on both your part and your partner's.

I'm not saying you have to get *Fifty Shades of Grey* kinky, but you should be actively engaging in foreplay, games, and positions your partner enjoys. Of course, they should return the favor to you, as well. And it's not just about sex. Keeping the spice alive in a long-term relationship is about intimacy, friendship, and expressing gratitude for one another.

Find Things That Make You Both Laugh

There's nothing as powerful as laughter. It bonds us as humans. It relieves stress. Laughter provides an instant dose of joy. The humor you create with your partner enhances your satisfaction with each other. Find movies, jokes, comedians, and types of humor that appeal to both of you. Bonding over laughter increases your appreciation for your partner. Be playful with each other, too. If you're playing and laughing together, there's really nothing that'll beat that kind of bond.

Be an Active Listener

The longer we're with a partner, the less we tend to listen. Am I alone in this? Don't lie to me, people! Listening to understand instead of listening to respond is so unbelievably difficult, and if you disagree, then I don't ever want to talk to you again. One way to make your love feel wanted and appreciated is to actually listen to them. Really pay attention, which means putting down your phone, looking them in the eye, and trying to understand what they're saying without simultaneously forming a response in your mind. This isn't easy to do. If you're like me, your instinct is to interrupt with your "superior" thought or a good joke. Try to contain yourself and let your partner finish their thought before you bust in with yours.

Flirt with Each Other and Continue to Date

The best part about new relationships is the dating and passion. Obviously, over time, that fades, but don't let the fire go out completely. I don't think we ever stop wanting our partners to flirt with us. Everyone longs to feel wanted. Flirting is fun, too.

It's cliché at this point to say, "Don't stop dating your spouse." I roll my eyes every time I hear this. Still, these annoying people who use too many quotes in their Facebook statuses are right. You should continue to date your spouse. Maybe once a month plan a romantic evening alone. Let your partner know that, even though time has passed and you've both put on a few pounds, you're still into them.

Do Fun Activities Together and Go on Adventures

We are humans and we are made to explore. Nothing will bring you closer to your partner than going on a fun adventure together. Spend some time in nature with your loved one. Studies show that the amount of time you spend in nature impacts your level of happiness. The more time you spend in the great outdoors, the happier you'll be. So why not bring the one you love along? Get out there and makes some memories together.

Be Open-Minded About New Sex Stuff

I think couples who've been married for years stop having sex because they are bored by the monotony. Or, maybe they're just old and have a decreased sex drive? Either way, no sex leads to resentment and will even further decrease your urge to get down and dirty. It's important to keep an open mind about sexual positions, foreplay, role-playing, and whatever the hell else you can think of. If your relationship is worth it, you'll be willing to switch it up every now and again. Of course, don't do anything you really don't want to try.

Operate Independently Together

A co-dependent relationship is bound to fail. You've got to be your own person. I like to call it "operating independently together." I know I just told you to have sex and go on cool adventures with your loved one, but you also need time to yourself. Space is not always a bad thing. You need your time alone as much as your partner deserves time to themselves, as well. In fact, I really think spending time apart will help you more genuinely appreciate your time together.

Be Kind, Forgiving, and Grateful...Especially When It's Difficult

When I feel personally attacked I instinctively resort to snarky comments and cheap shots. It's a terrible habit. I always regret resorting to this tactic. It only makes me feel worse knowing I hurt someone I care about. We could all stand to be a little more kind, forgiving, and grateful. When we're in an argument with our long-term partner or spouse, we reach a level of comfort that can make us unafraid to hurt the person we love. If you've been with the same person for years, it's not hard to take your partner for granted. That safety and security we find with a long-term relationship is a double-edged sword. On one hand, it's great to know they won't leave you over trivial matters. On the other hand, we get lazy in our loving and fighting. I think this explains why we sometimes treat the people closest to us worse than strangers. When I notice this in myself, I try to remember why I'm grateful for those I love. I also try to forgive them and myself for past wrongdoings.

I don't think monogamy has to be monotonous. Long-term

relationships take work, but sharing your life with a partner you love unconditionally is one of the most rewarding aspects of life. We crave these deep relationships so much we created *The Bachelor* and *The Bachelorette* TV shows.

How Do You Know if You're Ready for Marriage?

Raise your hand if you've ever asked: "How do you know if you're ready for marriage?" I think the answer lies somewhere between "I just knew he/she was the one" and "You're never 100% sure." There is no one-size-fits-all answer.

While I can't tell you if Sam is the person you should marry, I will give you a few questions to discuss with your partner if you're moving closer to tying the knot:

Have You Talked About Your Financial Situations (Honestly)?

Statistics don't lie. Most divorces come by way of financial disagreement. Honesty and transparency regarding your money and debt situation is crucial before entering into a union with someone. Before you put a ring on it, make sure to have an honest and earnest conversation about what you owe, what you own, and how you'll handle finances, together. You should know how much your partner makes, how many credit cards they're carrying, and how the bills will get paid each month after you're married. Get this shit figured out in advance and it'll make the transition to married life a little less stressful.

Have You Discussed Children, Religion, Career Goals, and Life Goals?

Oh, these are big ones. Don't marry someone if you don't know their desires, values, and hopes for the future. Don't wait to ask your partner if they want children until after you're married. If you discover one of you is on the baby train and the other has no intention of stepping foot into the baby station, it'll cause resentment and strain in your relationship. It's a little easier to compromise on religion (sometimes), career, and life goals, but knowing where your future spouse stands on these issues is part of the foundation of your life together. It's not easy to have frank discussions about sensitive topics. In fact, I'd rather gouge my eyes out than have most of these talks, but it's better to discuss them now than suffer the consequences later.

Are You Happy With Yourself?

So, why is being happy with yourself an important question to ask? Well, because if you aren't happy, it's a lot harder to make anyone else happy. If you aren't happy right now, what makes you think adding a lifelong commitment to another person is the answer? No one can fill your personal voids. In order to have a successful marriage, you both need to enter the union as complete individuals. You need to operate successfully independent of one another as self-reliant, mature, and fully developed human beings before you're truly ready to make such a serious commitment.

Why Do You Want to Get Married?

When I ask people, "Why do you want to get married?" a lot of times they haven't thought much past the point of "Because we love each other!" Do you want to get married because you've been together a long time? Or, because all your friends are getting married? Do the words "shit or get off the pot" come out of your family's mouth when referring to your relationship? I'm guessing, for the majority of us who've been in long-term relationships, at least one of these questions has popped up.

Marriage is about a lot more than love. Let me remove all the romance out of it for a moment and remind you: marriage is a legally binding contract. Marriage includes assets, liabilities, taxes, estates, and a myriad of other strings. It is not to be entered into lightly, because frankly, it isn't easy to get out.

I'm sure you love each other, but do you understand the benefits and pitfalls of marriage as a legal contract? Do you know how your finances and taxes will be affected? Do you

141

understand how expensive your rustic barn wedding theme is? Be sure you do, before you say, "I do." Don't rush into marriage. Take it seriously and see past your lust and love for one another. Marriage is more than a religious, spiritual, traditional, and romantic endeavor. If you view your lifelong commitment in more practical terms, you'll hopefully make a more informed decision when you decide to take the plunge into holy matrimony.

Are There Any Red Flags That Need Addressing?

Do not, I repeat, do not ignore or deny red flags in your relationship. You might be able to sweep them under the rug for the first few years of marriage, but eventually those red flags will reappear. There are hundreds of red flags: controlling behavior, a lack of trust, friends and family don't like your partner, secretive or manipulative actions, and of course any kind of emotional or physical abuse are all included. A partner who displays any of these behaviors may at times hide them or tell you they are trying to change. Be wary of people like this. Instead of sweeping red flags under the rug, sweep them out the door.

If you've addressed all pre-wedding questions and you're certain you're in love and ready to spend a lifetime with your partner, then go ahead and get married. Please let me know ahead of time if your wedding will include an open bar. If there is any doubt in your mind about marriage, communicate your concerns with your partner before proceeding. We tend to forget marriage isn't about the fancy wedding or the gorgeous dress. It's a contract in which you are legally combining your life with another human. Sure, your wedding day should be one of the happiest days of your life, but a wedding is not a marriage.

Oh, and one more thing. Don't go crazy planning your wedding. People only care about the food and music, the rest is just icing on the cake.

Thirty and Thriving

Your twenties only last ten years. Mathematically, we all
know this, but it's challenging to face the reality your
twenties will come to an end before you're ready. When I
turned 30, I cried. I stood in my shower the morning of my
birthday and I shed a tear. How did thirty years go by so fast?
I remember when my mom turned thirty. She was so much
more mature. I still view myself as a much younger person.
Christ, only 13 years ago I was in high school goofing off
with my friends. I still goof off with those same friends,
except now we have responsibilities and we've matured
from Boone's Farm wine to the much higher class BotaBox.
Thirty in the 21st century looks a lot different than in my
parents' and their parents' generations. Maybe it's because we
expect to live longer. Maybe it's because we aren't feeling the
same societal pressures. Maybe it's because we're aspiring to
different goals. I'm honestly not sure what makes thirty in
2017 so much different than 1987, '77, '67, and so on.
My mom also told me her 30s were some of the happiest
times of her life. I had a pretty good time in my twenties,
but I'm really hoping my thirties will be utilized a little
more wisely. I've spent a considerable amount of time
trying to figure out how to make the most of my thirties and
I've come up with a list to help us all thrive in this decade.

Be Honest About What You Want

As I entered my thirties, it was very clear that my life was
passing by faster than I anticipated. Time often feels like it's
speeding up as we get older. For a while, I let this bring me
down and I took on a very morbid what-does-it-matter-we'll-
all-be-dead-soon attitude. I dropped that after I realized
literally no one wants to hang out with someone who is
constantly consumed by their mortality. So, I tried to take a
different approach and let my aging body motivate me to
figure out what it is I really want. What do I value? What do
I want to accomplish? Who do I want to spend my time

with? The answers will shape my choices in my thirties and beyond.

Start Being Grateful

You've heard it a thousand times. Gratitude cultivates happiness. Honestly though, it's impossible to be grateful all the time. I'm a cynical bitch when I wake up in the morning. I cannot give thanks before 9 A.M. and a bold cup of coffee. Oprah and everyone on her *Super Soul Sunday* programs keep telling me to be grateful for the things I have, so I decided to make a conscious effort to give thanks at least once per day. At times it's not easy, but I think the trick is to remind yourself to be grateful during your worst moments. For whatever reason, whether it's God or Oprah or some higher power, giving thanks in a moment of weakness or sadness truly helps.

Nourish Your Relationships

I always want to be honest in my writing. So, I'm going to tell you I suffer from anxiety and depression (I know, I know, you're probably rolling your eyes). I don't expect pity. I just want you to know I'm one of the several millions of Americans who struggle with mental health. What I've found over the years is that nourishing the relationships in my life helps tremendously in battles against anxiety and depression. Cherished relationships and friendships will build you up when you've crumbled down.

Feed Your Brain

When I left for college my grandma said one sentence to me that I'll never forget. She said, "Don't come back thinking you know everything." That really stuck with me. I find I'm the most youthful and valuable as a human when I'm learning something new. I'm smart enough to know I don't know anything at all. I think the political divide in our country is partly because people aren't willing to admit they don't know things. Far too frequently when we don't know something, we either deny its existence and/or stand on the side of ignorance.

We've let our inflated egos build a wall preventing us from learning and understanding concepts outside our comfort zone.

Continuing to learn throughout your life is the path to wisdom, tolerance, and peace in your community and in your own soul. I know this sounds like some guru bullshit, but there isn't a person on this earth with all the answers. So, go read a book. Read an article from start to finish. Read things written by people you don't agree with. Read. Read. Read. Learn. Learn. Learn.

Do What You Love

When I say, "Do what you love." I'm not necessarily saying "Quit your job and go water ski for the next 20 years." Unfortunately, you can't always do what you love. So, even if you only "like" your job, find time before or after work, or on the weekends to do what you love. Self-care is important and partaking in an activity you adore at some point in the week is healthy for you.

Stop Giving a Shit About What People Think

You're in your thirties now, which means you've officially earned the right to stop caring what other people think. I decided to not care at age 29 when I finally decided to pursue comedy and writing. Why did I waste so many years worrying about embarrassing myself or wondering what people I cared about would say? Why did it matter so much to me? The day I decided to stop giving a shit was the first day of my sketch acting class in Atlanta. It was the best decision I ever made. I haven't looked back. It's made me a more confident and fulfilled person.

Your 30s are about really accepting and understanding yourself. Don't be afraid to unleash the best version of you.

Slayers of Single

You know what pisses me off more than almost anything? I hate it when society makes people who are single feel bad about it. If you're single, don't you waste one more second worrying about finding a partner. Continue to focus on yourself, your personal happiness, and the relationships already present in your life. Let me scream it so the folks in the back can hear, "Single people are fine and don't need your unsolicited opinions!"

Too often I hear older people say, "It's time for her to meet someone." I understand their sentiment of not wanting their loved ones to be lonely, but wish they would stop making assumptions about other people's lives. Like, how do you know it's time for them to meet someone? Are you Rafiki at the end of *The Lion King* whispering to Simba "It is time?" Get the fuck out of here.

Let's be real: it's most often parents who want their adult children to fall in love, get married, and give them grandchildren to spoil. But, applying that kind of pressure is not productive nor is it solicited. Why do we make single people feel as if they aren't enough in their current state?

Also, you can't force love. It'll happen when it happens, and if it doesn't happen, that's fine too. Perhaps the relationships already present in their life are enough. Shut it down, grandma!

Allow yourself to slay being single. I know plenty of people who own their singleness. There are numerous perks to being single. Here are few of the top reasons to embrace the single life:

You Can Do What You Want, When You Want

Freedom, baby, freedom. If you are single, savor that motherfucking freedom. Do the things you enjoy and savor every second you don't have to answer to anyone but yourself.

Focus on You

When I say, "focus on you," I'm talking about your mental health, your physical well-being, and your overall satisfaction in life. Take this time as a single person to figure yourself out. Who are you and who do you want to become? What makes you smile? What makes you tick? There's nothing sexier than someone who sincerely knows who they are in this world.

Your Happiness

Your happiness will increase in direct proportion to how much you focus on yourself. When you're happy, you're at your best. The world wants to see the optimum version of you, too. As a single person, you have the power to fill your life with things that bring you joy. Right now, you don't have to compromise on the movies you watch, music you listen to, and the time spent engaging in your favorite activities. What a blessing. Let your happiness grow.

A Good Night of Sleep

Humans were not made to sleep in the same bed together. I'm sorry if I'm a weirdo for thinking this. There's nothing worse than having to sleep next to someone who snores, tosses and turns, or gets up to go to the bathroom 18 times a night.

Basically, what I'm saying is you never want to share a bed with me. For real, you don't want to sleep next to me. I also fart in my sleep. When you're single, you can enjoy that big comfy bed all to yourself and not worry about your silently-but-deadly midnight slips.

Nurture Your Friendships

If you've got a great group of friends, you might be alone, but you'll never be lonely. Society tells single people they are relationship-less, but we all know that's not true. Friendships are relationships, and they need to be cherished. When you're single, take the time to nourish the relationships already present in your life. These people will be there to celebrate your triumphs and pick you up when your life falls apart. There's nothing more beautiful than a handful of close lifelong friends.

Low Maintenance Lifestyle

Grooming, pizza, and cleaning. You have options when you are single. Obviously, you don't have to completely bail on your hygiene or neglect your health, but if you don't shave for a couple of weeks, more power to you. Ladies, if you are single in the middle of winter, do not shave your legs. Let yourself experience the freedom of not having to groom. It is liberating. I would assume this is the same for guys and facial hair, but I'm not going to pretend I know about man hair. Can I make a totally random, not at all related to my life observation right now? You really don't appreciate how much hair you have on your butthole until you get it waxed for the first time. You know I'm right. The more I think about this shaving and waxing situation, the more I want to amend my previous statement. So, let me revise: If you are single, in a relationship, or married there's no reason to shave or wax in the winter. Did I just start a revolution?

Let me make this as clear as possible: your relationship status does not define who you are as a person. You are amazing and have so much to offer. You are enough on your own, I don't care how many people say to you, "It's time to meet someone," or, "When are you going to give us grandbabies?" This is your life, and your life alone. It is not for anyone to comment on.

The Most Important Relationship You'll Ever Have

If I told you you're already in the best relationship of your life, would you believe me? This relationship is rewarding, fulfilling, and characterized by love and positivity. What if I told you the greatest relationship you'll ever have is with yourself?

A few years ago, I wouldn't have believed me either. Learning to love yourself is a long journey, filled with plenty of self- doubt and self-criticism. We frequently forget no two people are the same. You are literally unique from any other person on this planet. Isn't that remarkable? So why the hell do we so hate ourselves so much? We're inherently different and special. There's no one on this planet who looks like you, thinks like you, acts like you, or has lived your experience. You are no better than anyone else, but more importantly, you are no worse. You can't begin to have success in money, career, and relationships until you can accept this fact.

One thing I've learned through therapy and reading an ungodly amount of self-help books is that how you perceive yourself is, most likely, far more negative than how the world actually views you.

Take Care of Your Mind

When I first started going to therapy, I was skeptical. I didn't know how or if it could help. I didn't believe talking to some guy, who doesn't know me, would improve my mental health. But, I gave it a chance anyway. By our fifth session, I started seeing improvement in my everyday life. My symptoms of depression and anxiety were still present, but their daily impacts lessened in severity. Of course, I still have my bad days and weeks, but therapy worked for me and I'm glad I put a priority on my mental health. We need to remove the stigma behind mental health. When I told family and friends I was in therapy for anxiety and depression, I was shocked to find out the majority of the people in my life were also seeking professional help. I wish I had known this earlier. I wish I could've been a better family member and friend during their struggles. We should encourage each other to seek help when needed. We shouldn't have to hide it like there's something wrong with us if we seek counseling. Not everyone has the luxury of seeing a therapist or psychiatrist, though. So, what can you do to take care of your mind on a daily basis? Personally, I love to read self-help books. Some are great, some are super cheesy, but nonetheless, I've checked out dozens from libraries. There's also many great podcasts that address mind and spirit. Try *The Tim Ferriss Show*, *The Hilarious World of Depression*, *Happier* with Gretchen Rubin, or *Therapy Chat*.

Take Care of Your Body

I despise going to the gym. I do it anyway. I'm not saying I'm better than the next person who decided to skip their workout today, but I know myself and I know how my symptoms of depression and anxiety are elevated when I don't workout. I go to the gym because I've become very aware of how much it affects my well-being physically and mentally. When I don't work out for just a few days, I can feel the energy drain from my body. I can feel myself slipping into bad eating habits and negative thoughts. For me, attending a class or going for a run puts a stop to this downward spiral and helps me be the best version of myself. I still hate working out, but I hate my out-of- shape, lethargic, and depressed nature more.

Of course, make sure you're eating a healthy diet and getting all the nutrients your body requires. There are thousands of resources from books to the Internet to help us develop a complete and healthy diet. Don't ever do those stupid fad diets or detoxes, though. I'm no dietician or nutritionist, but I know those are temporary fixes and not long-term healthy lifestyles.

If You Want to Give Love, Give It to Yourself First

The need to give and receive love is in our human nature. On occasion, we're so desperate for love we give our affection and attention to the wrong people. This happens the most when we forget to love ourselves first.

Healthy relationships are born from self-love. You must develop a positive relationship with yourself before you can find the love you deserve. A romantic partner will never be able to fill a void within your soul. So, work on yourself first before giving parts of your heart away.

Oh, wow, that got deep. I'm over here acting like Elizabeth Gilbert. I'm just eating, praying, and loving my way through this life. Emphasis on eating.

Learn from the Past, but Don't Regret It

I've made more than a few mistakes in my life. I'd say drunkenly falling out of a cab in Las Vegas and subsequently breaking my nose on the curb is pretty high on the list. I've also been a jerk to friends, passive-aggressive in relationships, and in high school I used to prank call people all…the…time. Do I regret any of it? At this point in my life, no I don't. I wish I made better decisions, but I did learn a lesson from each of my mistakes and I think I'm a better person now for it.

Of course, we've all done worse than high school prank calls, but I think it's important we forgive ourselves. Life is too short, and our transgressions are bigger in our heads than they are in real life. Apologize when it's necessary, do better next time, but forgive yourself for being human. We're all idiots.

Congratulations on Getting Your Shit Together!

Thank you for reading this book. Before you go, I want to give you a quick pep talk. So here goes: life is confusing and unpredictable. Being an adult can really suck and you're going to have to overcome a lot of adversity. We all have our own challenges and obstacles. I'm sorry life has to be this way. It's unfortunately and unfairly even more difficult for marginalized communities. There are injustices and circumstances which are systemic and, at times, insurmountable. I don't have an answer for that other than that we all need to continue to work together to lift each other up and end inequality and all the various forms of - isms.

With that being said, you are still accountable to yourself and there are small steps you can take to improve your life. Whether that's creating a budget, opening a savings account, or picking the right student loan repayment plan. Do what you can to put yourself in the best position for the future. It won't always be easy, and I haven't provided all the answers for you in this collection of essays, but you can fucking do this.

You will survive, and better yet, you will thrive. How do I know this? Well first of all, you just finished reading a book about personal finance, career, and relationships, which tells me you're serious about getting your shit together. You are aware you don't have all the answers, and you know there are resources out there that can teach and help you. Don't be afraid to ask for assistance along the way. I'll say it one more time: be smart enough to know you don't know anything at all. You don't have to become an expert in personal finance or career building to be a successful person. Arm yourself with the fundamentals and know where to look for answers. You're going to run into personal and professional issues that'll stump you — even after the massive amount of knowledge I'm sure you've acquired from this book — so be sure to put your ego to the side and utilize your resources until you find an answer.

It's okay to make mistakes and fail. There is no greater learning tool than failure. When you're at your lowest point following a mistake or defeat, remember to find the lesson. There's always something to learn. I promise you won't absorb nearly as much useful information from your successes as you will from your failures. Start to view failure as a necessity to achieving greatness.

Right now, from this moment on, I don't ever want you to give another flying fuck what "people might think." When we're all dead and gone, what is it going to fucking matter if your friends thought you were weird for taking an improv class? Or, if you pursued art? Or, if you were unsuccessful in entrepreneurship? It's not going to matter. What matters is that you tried. I promise you your headstone won't say, "I hope those girls I used to have brunch with still think I'm cool." Well they don't, because they aren't thinking about you, probably because they're dead too. Also, guess what? People aren't obsessing about what you're doing with your life. Chances are your friends are wondering what you're thinking about them as much as you are. So, why don't we try a new approach and stop worrying about the perceived thoughts of our family, friends, and acquaintances to focus on pursuing our interests and passions?

On average, we have about 85 years to live on this planet. That's it. One lifetime, that's all you get. So go balls to the walls as often as you can and chase your dreams without letting any comments from the peanut gallery derail you. I'm serious. Go after what you want and don't ever fucking stop. If you fall short, you won't regret failing as much you'll regret not trying.

Before I release you back into the world, I have one secret to tell you. There's no such thing as "having your shit together." No, you didn't waste your time reading this book. What I mean is that you can have it together in certain

153

aspects of your life, but really we all continue to struggle in various areas. As my best friend Jessie once told me, "Everybody's got their issues."

She was right. We're all on this continuous journey to get our shit together and then somehow keep it together.
Just like you, I'm going to spend the rest of my life trying to get it together, but I guess that's half the fun.

Resources and Links

1. FINRAInvestor Education Foundation, "National Financial Capability Study," 2016, http:// www.usfinancialcapability.org

2. Prudential, "Financial Experience and Behaviors Among Women," 2014-2015, http:// www.prudential.com/media/ managed/wm/media/ Pru_Women_Study_2014.pdf

3. National Network to End Domestic Violence, "About Financial Abuse," accessed July 31, 2017, http:// nnedv.org/ resources/ejresources/about-financial-abuse.html

4. Center for American Progress, "Women's Economic Risk Exposure and Savings," April 27, 2017, https:// www.americanprogress.org/issues/economy/reports/ 2017/04/27/431228/womens-economic-risk-exposure-savings/

5. Jillian Berman, "America's Growing Student Loan Debt Crisis," *MarketWatch*, January 19, 2016, www.marketwatch.com/story/americas-growing-student-loan- debt-crisis-2016-01-15

6. To learn more about stocks: "Stock," *Investopedia*, accessed July 31, 2017, http://www.investopedia.com/terms/ s/stock.asp

7. To learn more about bonds: "Bond," *Investopedia*, accessed July 31, 2017, www.investopedia.com/terms/b/ bond.asp

8. To learn more about mutual funds: "Mutual Fund," *Investopedia*, accessed July 31, 2017, www.investopedia.com/ terms/m/mutualfund.asp

9. To learn more about Traditional and Roth IRAs:"Traditional IRA vs. Roth IRA," *Investopedia*,

accessed July 31, 2017, www.rothira.com/traditional-ira-vs-roth-ira

10. To learn more about pensions: "Pension Plan," *Investopedia*, accessed July 31, 2017, www.investopedia.com/ terms/p/pensionplan.asp

11. A good article on common stock plan mistakes: "Six Employee Stock Plan Mistakes to Avoid," *Fidelity*, June 8, 2016 https://www.fidelity.com/viewpoints/stock-plan-mistakes

12. Here's some more information on what to do with your old savings bonds: Qiana Chavaia, "6 Smart Ways to Use Old Savings Bonds," December 30, 2014, http:// www.wisebread.com/6-smart-ways-to-use-old-savings-bonds

13. For more on 401k's check out: "401(k) Plan," accessed July 31, 2017, http://www.investopedia.com/terms/ 1/401kplan.asp

14. To find out what tax bracket you're in: US Tax Center, "2016 Federal Tax Rates, Personal Exemptions, and Standard Deductions: IRS Tax Brackets & Deduction Amounts for Tax Year 2016," accessed July 31, 2017, https://www.irs.com/ articles/2016-federal-tax-rates-personal-exemptions-and- standard-deductions

15. Here's a cool calculator to do the federal income tax math for you: "Federal Tax Brackets," *moneychimp*, accessed July 31, 2017, http://www.moneychimp.com/ features/ tax_brackets.htm

16. Electronic Federal Tax Payment System (for estimated taxes): https://www.eftps.com/eftps/

17. Direct Pay system (a little easier to use to pay estimated taxes): https://www.irs.gov/payments/direct-pay

17. Amy Cuddy TED: *Your Body Language May Shape Who You Are*, June 2012, https://www.youtube.com/watch?v=Ks-_Mh1QhMc

Acknowledgements

I want to thank the people who were instrumental throughout this process. I apologize, I know there's people I'm forgetting, but I just got done writing a book and I'm exhausted. Cut me some freaking slack, you guys. Here are a few people who do deserve some extra love:

To my editor, Tiffany Vann Sprecher, thank you for your guidance and impeccable editing skills. Your help in this process was invaluable. I'm grateful to the internet Gods for bringing us together.

My book cover designer, Erin Nausin. Thank you for understanding my weird vision and turning it into a true piece of art.

To everyone at *The Scold*, without you I wouldn't have a book. Thank you for the opportunity to freely rant about the topics that mean the most to me: financial literacy, feminism, and fantasy football.

To my parents and sister who never thought my dreams were too big or crazy: thank you for your unconditional support. Everything I do is to make you proud. Less than three.

Daniel, thank you for keeping me focused, for pushing me when I think I can't go any further, and for loving me when I'm annoying as hell. You are an American hero in every sense of the word.

To my N.A. Crew, thank you for making me laugh every single day. You all know I'm crazy, but you stick by my side anyway. I'm lucky to have such wonderful friendships in my life.

Oprah. I can't forget Oprah Winfrey. I've been a lifelong

lifelong fan. I'm hoping by mentioning you in my acknowledgements you'll feel compelled to invite me to your home on Maui. If not, lunch sometime? I'll pay!

Let's Be Friends!

Twitter!

@CatieHogan
@GetItTogether20
@Hogan_Financial

Facebook!

@CatieHoganWrites
@HoganFinancialPlanning

My Podcast!

"Get It Together with Catie Hogan" is available on iTunes and SoundCloud:
https://itunes.apple.com/us/podcast/get-it-together-with-catie- hogan/id1247294531?mt=2

Instagram!

@catie_hogan20